# Honour Your Calling

## The Professional's Guide to
## Quitting Your Job
## and Doing
## Your Soul Work.

## by Angelyn Toth

XENIACREATIONS.COM

# Foreword

Honour your Calling comes at a time when the world seems to be falling apart and confusion reigns. You may feel like your life and work are falling apart and you may feel confused as to what direction to go in. I know exactly what you're going through. I used to have a safe and secure job as a wildlife biologist in the federal government of Canada. After about a decade, I became deeply depressed because my soul was unfulfilled doing that work. I felt like my soul was dying.

After many years of struggle and finally making a spiritual breakthrough, I discovered my life purpose and vision and became one of the pioneers in the 1990s of the "creating the work you love by learning how to listen to your spiritual gifts, your heart, intuition and psychic gifts. I finally found my calling. Oh how I wish that I had had Angelyn Toth's book "Honour your Calling" to shortcut the multi-year process. It would have saved me years of pain, wasted time and energy doing a job that I no longer loved and struggling to find what I did love.

In Honour your Calling, Angelyn offers you hope, inspiration and simple tools from her own life and those of her clients to release patterns of self-sabotage that you may be experiencing as a result of limiting beliefs about yourself. When you have limiting beliefs, it's impossible to find the dream of your work, let alone create it and honour your Calling.

By generously sharing her journey, trials and tribulations and the way she gracefully resolved them, Angelyn provides you with a roadmap and tools to solve your immediate pains and challenges that you might be experiencing now......and will experience in the process of honouring your calling. Now you have the opportunity to learn from a master.

Both Angelyn and the land of Xenia have changed the lives of thousads through her silent retreats, and programs on Honouring your Calling. This book, Honour your Calling is an invitation for you to truly step into your life and your dream of work. I guarantee when you do you'll feel excited, inspired and fulfilled on every level, physical, mental, emotional and spiritual. And your life will be filled with even greater joy and love doing what you came here to do, what you were meant to do.

You're at a pivotal moment in your life. You want to make an incredible leap to do what's in your heart of hearts!! Honour your Calling offers you an invitation and bridge to give you clarity to doing the most meaningful work of your life. I hope you accept the invitation. You'll never regret it!!

**Ellen Hayakawa** *(www.EllenHayakawa.com) Author of "The Inspired Organization: Spirituality and Energy at Work," Co-Author of Amazon Best Seller and Best Inspirational Spiritual Book of the Year: "Healing the Heart of the World: Harnessing the Power of Intention to Change your Life and Your Planet"*

# Acknowledgements

There are many people I wish to acknowledge beginning with my daughter, Kasara Toth. She has been my inspiration when I wonder if I can achieve something. She has role modelled going for your dreams and today she is an equine veterinarian and lives every day in her passion with horses. She was like a straight arrow once she knew what she wanted to do.

Next, Chrystalle Grace who was the first person I ever felt witnessed by. She continues to support me with her grace, from the world beyond. I would like to thank her sister, Diane Leclair who bugged me for years to get this book done. To Saria Suzan Bailey, for her patience and radical trust of me, Xenia, and our global program.

Ariel Cantin, my inspiration for this book and long-time friend and soul sister. Elinor Meney who for years has coached me through blocks and limitations standing in my way to fully showing up in the world. Ellen Hayakawa, my friend and soul sister, for many assignments and writing buddy. To Renee Beth Poindexter for seeing a bigger vision for me and tenaciously helping me see it too. I want to mention Marina Richards for many years of friendship and adventures into the deep world of transformation.

And last but not least, Alexander Brumm who showed up in my life at the perfect time, in the ideal way. I love our journey together and sharing a common purpose.

# Introduction

*"Take one step towards the Gods, and they will take ten steps towards you. - Joseph Campbell.*

I was inspired to write this book for you, who have a dream on your heart yet to be fulfilled. My crusade is to encourage as many people as possible to live up to and honour their Calling.

Sharing my book recently with a friend at a local coffee shop, he asked, "Does a person have to honour their Calling?"

To which I replied, "Absolutely not!" I went on, "This is simply an invitation for those who are ready and feel the resonance in my words. I am not interested in any shoulds or guilt trips about this, but more an inspiration and connection if it applies to you. Maybe you are already doing this in which case pass it on to someone you think may enjoy it. Or maybe you will never ever be interested in this lifetime. No worries. You probably wouldn't have even picked this book up if that was the case. But if you are holding this book in your hands and you do not know why, STOP, WAIT ... be curious enough to check it out because maybe a deeper soulful part of you has guided you here.

I personally took this step many years ago and found a way to fund my movement, which included buying a 38-acre dilapidated sheep farm and transforming it into a beautiful retreat centre. Twenty-five years later it is a global centre, receiving guests from all over the world. From there the journey continued and today I am grateful beyond measure to be living my Soul work every day in everything I do. I want this for you too if you are not already honouring your Calling.

The most important aspect of this journey is to touch deeply, the essence of your soul. Feeling within and listening to what life is showing you in each sacred moment. Life speaks to all of us every day and all-day long. You can safely know there is a higher power guiding you if you can simply tune in and act upon its messages.

Our Soul work can be two-fold. First it is the work we must do to deliver the gifts with which we were born. This may include moving obstacles out of the way and shifting perspective on what is possible from a new vantage point. And, second, it is the way we work in the world by way of vocation, volunteering and contributing in a variety of different ways.

This book stirs up the part that knows the way and summons you forth into your awakening. Each page is packed with provocative enquiry and it may well cause you to be inspired, tired, or even emotional. One thing for sure it will move you towards that which is calling you.

Understanding what is calling to you, is only the beginning. The next steps will be the action you take towards your Soul. You may need to take many breaks to ponder the questions being asked throughout this book. There may be many areas you relate to and some you will not. I suggest you stay open to all possibilities presented in these words. Journal what arises throughout the chapters. Imagine living the life you were meant to live. One where your soul wakes up every morning, stretches and goes about its day. Unlike our conditioned, programmed ego mind who tells stories of what we must do; what is right and what is wrong. What if there were no such thing as limitations and you were free to create your life the way you see fit.

This urgency of respect towards our Soul work happens usually a bit later in life. When you have lived many years and many experiences. What if it could happen sooner than later? What if what you have to offer is important to the world. Not only to your world but to all the people you touch when you are living your authentic life.

It may not be a change in "job" or profession, instead it may be about adding this Soul work into your life while you become a master of delegation. Freeing up time and space to give attention to your Soul Work.

Follow all the way through the book and look at relationships and how they can impact you greatly towards your success with your Soul work. And most importantly the love of Self which is what, true Soul work, is really all about.

Come to the end of the book and discover *it is all handled*. Everything, all of it and all you have to do is show up. Are you ready? If so, I invite you to embark on this journey with me.

# CHAPTER ONE

# What is Your Calling?

*"There is no greater gift you can give or receive than to honor your Calling"* —Oprah Winfrey

Your Calling is that which calls to you in the undercurrent of your life. You may be aware of what this is but haven't given yourself permission to proceed or you may not have been acquainted with what this is yet.

Are you feeling haunted by a deep yearning but don't actually explore it because something is holding you back? Even if you have lived a fulfilling career aligned with your Calling, do you assume it ends with your retirement?

You may feel done with your career and now it's time to do the work you really want to do. You have put in a lifetime doing the work you mastered and got a lot of praise for it. Boredom may have set in as you face the truth that you are done with it and long to do what is on your heart and yet to be expressed.

Maybe you have even fallen into apathy or depression from holding back your dream. In this book we will walk through a journey together to get clear about what is calling to you and what has created such hesitation in taking the leap of faith into this new world. Questions and thoughts you may have are:

- o Am I too old now to start again?
- o Does it really matter what I have to share?
- o What difference can I make?
- o What is my Calling anyway?
- o I don't know if I can make enough money doing what I love?
- o Nobody really cares what I have to offer.
- o How would I even begin?
- o I'm unsure about myself.
- o Maybe I should wait a little longer?

I don't know about you, but I grew up with a lot of: *Who do you think you are to want this or to do that?*

Now, in my more mature years, the story is more like: *What's the point, why bother, isn't it too late to do that?*

So, when is the right time to break free and do what you came to planet earth to do? Whose permission do you need to begin? Let's assume you have the go ahead and will find ways and means of accomplishing the dream on your heart. Are you curious as to why it hasn't happened yet and if it will.

Apart from asking yourself many questions that probably will crack open the light of awareness about your next chapter, I'm going to share with you a process that creates change at an instinctive level. And this means below the level of belief to a far deeper level. I will also be referring to other modalities to unearth the plan for your future and put you on the path of your Calling.

We will expose hidden saboteurs that devastate our chances of ever having a soul mission and actually living it. We will look at how un-forgiveness is a guarantee of separation and how in this state we can never fulfill our Calling. Also, we will see how surrender can only happen through acceptance and understanding and is actually not in your control. We will see how important love is and how to become conscious of your unconscious roadmap for love.

I say if not now when? In fact, the further along on your journey, the more qualified you are, and the more you have to offer from direct experience and accumulated skills. Our western culture unfortunately does not treasure the knowledge and wisdom available from our elders and most times you are seen and treated as less than and a burden as you age. If you're reading this book you're probably not ready to drop your cloak anytime soon, but you are aware of your body getting older.

The good news is, the best is yet to come and when you move beyond the enculturation you may have been assaulted with, you can choose again. You will discover the power of nature and of welcoming more silence into your life. It is within the silence you connect to your deeper truth.

Ideas will be given as to where and how to find silent retreats or just a way to carve out some solace time for yourself. Discover how to relate to nature and learn how useful and available it is to listen to your story. You will find peace and open pathways of awareness as you lean in and develop your trust.

And ultimately, to consider the idea: *it is all handled*, so you can relax into your life and witness the unfolding journey in each moment. Learning how life moves you, not the other way around. A beautiful surrender into radical trust and you are home. From this place you learn how your next step and contribution awaits you and gives you the message you are to deliver to the world. Imagine having that much help and learning what you have to share is so important. You are not old and spent and retired, you are fertile ground for awesomeness.

We will look at your levels of readiness and see if we can free up some room by eliminating things you think you want but actually do not. This open space becomes available for this new work and expansion towards your true Calling.

You may have to get uncomfortable enough to take action—that's right: uncomfortable. Usually until things are that way we do not act. Think about how long you have wanted to shift gears, but yet your car is idling fine in its present gear.

Until now, you may have been living the perfect life that you were meant to live and probably have made a big difference in many people's lives. And now here you are on the precipice of great change and it may feel scary. Don't worry. I'm here to walk through this with you.

Do you feel a stirring deep in your heart and you want to make a difference? Do you ever lie awake at night feeling something is missing? That there's something else you're supposed to be doing? Maybe feeling like you haven't ever really lived the life you wanted to live yet. You carry on with your commute to work the next day and do the job you have mastered, and life ticks on. Another day, another month, and another year.

Before you know it, another decade has passed you by and still no change has been made. What will it take to make the plunge into the unknown territory of your true Calling? How many more years are you willing to wait and live in resistance? What has not taking this step cost you? Maybe your health and joy?

In this book you will find the support needed to deeply investigate your longing and why you want to make this shift. Together we will get to the bottom of what it is you 'really' want and whether or not you are ready to do whatever it takes to get it done.

You will be guided and supported every step of the way because this is not something you can do alone. It takes having a support team to witness this step and hold you by the hand into your next life. Consider this:

o Have you lived your significance yet?

o Imagine being seen at this deepest level and acknowledged for what you have yet to bring to the world.

o Imagine freeing the inner spirit that wants to create or co-create in a new way.

o Imagine making a difference in a way that is beyond your wildest dreams because you bring with you your 10,000+ hours of experience and true alignment.

- Imagine it is your time now and the light just turned green.
- Imagine how you will feel when you are doing this work and in alignment with your soul.
- Imagine feeling fulfilled by the work you are doing.
- Imagine combining your passion with your contribution.
- Imagine the impact you can have with others when you take this bold step.

It takes courage to begin and radical trust to continue.

What this book is not:

- It is not about finding you a job or new career.
- It is not about inventing a purpose.
- It is not an ideology to follow.
- It's not about telling you what you should do next.

It is about creating an environment and space into which you will discover the answers for yourself. You are the one you are looking for and you are the one who has the answers.

If anything, we move "stuff" out of the way so you can see clearly what it is you want deep down.

There is nothing you have to fix to offer your gift to the world.

In a way, this book is about finding yourself at the deepest place possible. Not the titles you've worn like CEO, doctor, nurse, architect, etc. Beyond your roles as mother, father, teacher, and even beyond gender, color, and creed. Even beyond to the only place you will find peace and fulfillment and it will totally surprise you.

There is a place of stillness and tranquility within all of us and this book is an attempt to bring you there.

My hope is this book inspires you to find your own deep inner dream by truly witnessing the feelings arising and trusting the messages being given. You will discover your unique Calling and why it is time to share it.

You will notice three sections to my book based on OPA, Opening Pathways of Awareness. It is the name of the 90-Day Program we offer at my retreat centre and is the name of our beloved 1000-year-old

Douglas Fir tree where people come to visit from far and wide every year. When I first connected with the name OPA, I was surprised because I knew it meant grandfather in different languages. For me, the first time I heard the name of the tree, I interpreted the acronym right away as Opening Pathways of Awareness. This has become the subtle basis of the work I cherish and one we will be witnessing throughout this book. Let's begin with the first section.

# SECTION ONE

# Opening to Your God Given Gifts

In this opening section we look at what it is that is Calling to you and what is stopping you—or has stopped you—from going for it until now. We are opening up all possibilities to build a picture, so you can see clearly what you need to become aware of for change to happen. An open mind and heart are what we are looking for in this section and it is where you will find answers and allow the intelligence of consciousness to assist you.

A closed mind blocks our inspiration and ability to receive and for this reason I wanted to spend the next few chapters looking at why this is so important. What we want and why it hasn't happened is the subject of this section.

# CHAPTER TWO

# Longing to Break Free and Soar

*Definition of Calling: a strong inner impulse toward a
particular course of action especially when accompanied by
conviction of divine influence.* —Merriam-webster.com/dictionary

In this chapter we will make real the idea of
honouring your Calling now. And then take it
from an idea and look at ways of actualizing this
plan in the world. I have described two ways of
stepping across into your next career using stepping-
stones or literally jumping off the cliff into the pool
of opportunities.

You are in your essence when you are honouring
your Calling. It is your true north set out in front of
you when you let the divine influence you. When
you resist, it causes you to cling to plans that aren't
working, stick to jobs that are unfulfilling and obsess

over relationships that are not aligned. Sometimes we think our blocks are about not enough money, time, energy, or one of many other excuses. We will drill down on these excuses and learn they are not the problem once we have shifted our perspective. You will find out in the next chapters how to go beyond the restrictions of the mind and open to the power within.

Recently I woke up from one of those vivid dreams that stayed with me for weeks. In the dream I was in a jail in Hungary. It appeared to be hundreds of years ago. The jail was old and damp with a gully of water running through it. My sentence was long, and I felt like I was never getting out. The bars were made of thick metal and the walls were stone. Frantically, I pulled at the bars trying to dislodge them with all the strength I could muster. I was sweating and panicking as I pleaded for my life. Soon I understood I wasn't getting out because I didn't have the physical horsepower to break through the bars. My next thought was, okay, if that's the case and I cannot physically get myself out of here, I will have to think and strategize my way out. For quite a while I pondered this. What could I do? How could I receive help? Should I pray?

My mind was looking for answers when suddenly I became totally aware the prison was not outside of me at all. It was inside. In a blinding flash of truth, the walls literally dissolved before my very eyes into dust and I stepped out.

Waking up from this dream, I knew it was a prophetic message to help in areas of my life I had been struggling with. I started to inquire into my own self-created jail. Where was I pretending to be in jail and unable to move freely? What parts of my conditioning needed exposing and de-constructing? Over the following months I saw my clients and my team in similar circumstances in their own self-created jails. In many cases, they were without any awareness and didn't know how to move beyond this limitation I now knew, with certainty, didn't actually exist.

*The jail is an illusion that feels real.*

Are you done with your career energetically, emotionally, and truly? What once saved your life and served you greatly may now feel like it could kill you if you stay one more day. You have been doing an awesome job and your employers want you to stay on and even develop your role. They will give you more money or more shifts and you want to take it and please them and earn the extra income, but there is a big conflict inside. Every hour, week, and month you carry on this pathway, you feel like it is eating away at the possible time left to do the work of your soul. Maybe there is a legacy you want to leave behind for your family or a mission you feel strongly about contributing to. What is the passion knocking on the door of your soul? What is your Calling? How do you feel when you don't open the door and dismiss it as impossible?

Do you tend to agree with your mind that asks you to just relax and accept your destiny with the job you have? You are good at it and you're already established. You even consider it and do some therapy to reach a place of acceptance. Until one day you wake up with this yearning in your heart once again and you slump back down feeling out of integrity with your soul.

Many people are in this situation and very few actually break free and change direction.

*Are you in this predicament?*

Sometimes changing direction means creating a bigger team around you so you can do the parts of the job you enjoy and delegate the rest.

Many have already retired and are free to deliver more of who they are to the world, but they settle for mediocrity and life without passion. Or they do all the things expected of a retired person and have fun for a while. They feel relieved they have so much freedom to do whatever they want. Yet the one thing they are assigned to do is eclipsed by their fear and doubt.

*Could you be afraid by the lack of structure your retirement freedom has created?*

Recently one of my clients was staying at my retreat centre and we did quite a few sessions together. He is a retired medical doctor and after retirement did a lot of travelling around the world. Next, he downsized from an apartment in Seattle and home in Bellingham, to a small cottage on one of the San Juan Islands where he joined a community.

It was a devastating process for him as he let go of decades of memories and pain. He sounded like a tortured soul as we talked and he shared about how though he has all this time, he is lost and unsure of himself. As a doctor, he had his life purpose and loved serving in this way. He really felt at the time he was living his Calling. Now he is just a guy—an older guy at that. There was a big gap in his heart and his daily routine now that the structure around his career had collapsed. In spite of his successful career, he shared that he felt he hadn't really lived as himself yet. He didn't really know who he was beyond being a doctor. In other words, his retirement had totally disoriented him.

Most of the time he was panicked and afraid of really hearing his mind going on and on about this and that. I asked him to spend time in the Sanctuary and out in nature, which he did. He started to hear the worry of his mind and what its concerns were. By the time he left he was quiet, peaceful, and still.

Even though he had become present and open while he was in nature with support, his obsessive mind continued to haunt him as he returned to his life. His journey has just begun, but for now at least he knows the direction of his work, which is to arrest the constant barrage from his mind and find peace in his heart. Fortunately, he returned to attend a powerful program with Nancy Shipley Rubin[1] and made peace with his pain and opened like I had never seen before. He received tools that helped him stay awake and feel through his body by being grounded. I love witnessing transformation, and this is what I saw as he emerged out of his initial despair.

Opening and receiving is the way back to the heart and into the next steps. His Calling that lived through his career as a doctor did not go away and is always there. But what does it translate into now? This is his new quest. And now he is more prepared to discover his next steps.

**Back to you:**

What is the work of your soul?

Do you feel like a part of you has never really lived?

Are you ready to own it?

What do you need to get you there?

What do you need to let go of?

---

[1] www.rubinenterprises.info

What tools will help you in this process?

What examples are there to use as a roadmap?

What story have you been telling yourself?

Do you build a bridge or jump right in?

What kind of structure can you create to feel safe as you move forward?

When do you take this step?

These are important questions to ask yourself and in the next chapters, we will look at them all and get the answers you have been looking for.

JOURNAL WORK

Take time now to journal and answer the most important questions for you at this time.

What prison bars have you erected around yourself for protection?

Which of the questions in this chapter struck you at a deep level? Are there other questions you have about this time in your life and your journey? Questions are where we begin.

# CHAPTER THREE

# Exit Plan

In this chapter, I'll share two ways of making a big transition. See if one way speaks to you more than the other.

I wake up curious every day about what is on the schedule of the great divine plan. It wasn't always this way, but today I live in radical trust and implicit faith that there is a power greater than myself moving through me. This is definitely not a passive role, but you could say it's a co-creative way of living life and this is very much what my work is today. Throughout this book you will find me encouraging, nudging, and sometimes downright begging you to give your beautiful God Given Gift (GGG) to the world.

If you are in a job or career path you are tired of and your ambition and creation here has diminished, you may wonder how to get from A to B.

There were two times I would like to share specifically about how I exited from my job into the next steps of my journey. One was using the bridge method and the other was the total jumping off the cliff into the unknown method. Either way works— it depends on how urgent you feel about it and your circumstances at the time. Both times brought about deeper alignment with my Calling.

## THE BRIDGING EXIT:

I felt like a square peg in a round hole, longing for something deeper to fulfill me. I worked downtown at the Royal Bank corporate offices in advertising and while I had a fair bit of freedom in this unique department, I never felt like I was in my right work. Sure, it provided a job with a good salary, but I learned a lot about what I didn't want to do for the rest of my life.

Seven years of nine to five felt like a prison sentence to my soul. Working on the 35th floor of this big tower, it was way too far from the ground and especially from nature.

A few years later, a brochure came across my desk about a public speaking workshop. Like many people, this was my greatest fear. I would get red with embarrassment when speaking at a meeting with more than two-and-a-half people present. This impeded my growth and ability to share my ideas, so the course called to me. I asked my boss if they would pay for me to do the workshop because it would improve my ability to speak at meetings and, sure enough, they approved my request.

I have heard people say that a particular workshop changed their life and this was the one that did for me. Attending this program changed my life profoundly and put me on the path of my Calling. By the end of the weekend, I could stand up and speak without a red face or terror surging through my body. I learned how to think on my feet and become present to the audience. It felt surprising and transformational.

At the end, I asked the instructor, Harold, what it would take to lead this program. His precision with the process and the people struck me and the results were astounding. I was surprised how this question came out of me. I thought he would say it would take having a psychology degree.

The instructor looked at me intently and replied, "Well, you would make a great facilitator. If you want, I will teach you."

You should have seen the shock on my face when Harold made this offer. He was in his late seventies and had barely taught anyone how to lead his program, which seemed surprising given how brilliant it was. So, mentor me he did, in all the spare time I had outside of my bank job.

This whole area of transformation had grabbed me, and I couldn't get enough of it. I was a sponge sucking up everything I could to learn and I knew the trajectory of my life had radically changed.

I wanted to quit my job and go work in this new really fulfilling venture, but I was afraid to take the risk. I was earning good money and felt a responsibility to the company. After a year of struggling to get enough time to learn and take part in all the programs Harold was leading, I went to my boss at the Royal Bank and asked if I could go part-time. He said "no" right away because it wasn't customary back then, in the corporate culture (we're talking the 80s).

Never being good at taking no for an answer, I wrote a letter laying out a plan of how it would work by farming certain projects out to different departments. They would even save money, I added.

After one week of discussions, my proposition got accepted, and for the next two years, I worked part time with the Royal Bank and the rest of the time with Harold. My bridge was set, and I started crossing it.

I travelled with him to Toronto and worked with big corporations like IBM, Bank of Montreal, Vancouver Board of Trade, and many others. Very quickly I was leading eighty percent of the program.

One day on a flight, he confessed to me that he had never given a speech and it was his one cardinal rule. I asked why not, and he said, "You could get scrutinized and people may find fault. As a facilitator of this program, you don't want to set yourself up for that."

Boy, did that surprise me. All this time, I had imagined he must have given hundreds of speeches when in fact he had given none. He only taught and facilitated them. Well, that didn't sit right with me, and I decided to book some talks, so I could see if his theories worked in the real world.

The first speech I gave was at a Sales and Marketing breakfast meeting for a couple of hundred people. The perfect opportunity presented itself when I found out from a colleague that their assigned speaker had to cancel a couple of days before the event, and the organizer was desperate to find a replacement. Boldly, I offered my services. He said, "Are you sure? My neck is on the line here, and you have to be good." I assured him I would deliver, and he had no need to worry.

Over the next few days, I prepared the skeleton of my speech, taking in all the advice and training I had received, and did a lot of visualization. In my mind's eye, I saw the audience as attentive and leaning forward to listen. I saw swarms of people staying behind to talk to me after.

On the drive in the morning of the speech, I trembled with excitement and fear. Suddenly, I had to pull the car over and throw up because I felt so nervous. Doubt crept into my mind and I thought of running in the other direction but using all the skills I had, gathered up the courage and arrived at the event, poised and ready to participate.

Before stepping on stage, I managed to pull it together and, within minutes, I relaxed and became present with the audience. I noticed a fair bit of spontaneity in my talk, and an ease the further along I went. By the laughter in the room, I noticed I was naturally funny on my feet. Not with jokes, but by painting amusing scenarios people could relate to. It turned out I got rave reviews and dozens of people stood in line to talk to me afterward, just as I had visualized. The organizer said it had gone excellently, and he felt pleased. Phew, I'd pulled it off.

After that, I led corporate programs and gave talks to a variety of businesses and organizations. My life as a public speaker was launched, and I went from sheer terror in front of all sizes of audiences, to feeling natural and capable in most situations.

I had crossed the bridge to my next life and although it took a few years before I finally quit my job at the Royal Bank, it was the right way to go for me at the time.

This put me on the path of my deepest Calling that led to my purchasing an old broken down 38-acre sheep farm and transforming it into a beautiful retreat centre.

Again, my total passion was alive and happy.

## THE JUMPING OFF THE CLIFF EXIT:

After 10 years into the creation of my retreat centre, Xenia, we were suffering financially to the point where I hit some serious financial losses and was desperate to find a way to save my dream from going back to the bank. I was five months behind in the mortgage, three years behind in property taxes, there were disconnection notices, and I was beside myself in terror of losing my beloved Xenia. It was one of the lowest points in my life and led to months of fear and terror. This I refer to as my dark night of the soul and I will be sharing more about this is Chapter 8.

This awful situation led me to a business opportunity in relationship marketing. Highly skeptical of this approach to doing business, I had a lot of pre-conceived ideas that were seemingly justified from a previous brush with the sector some thirteen years earlier.

I held old-paradigm beliefs of what I thought it was and vowed I would never be foolish enough to get sucked into it again. So, when it reared its head, I said 'No' with absolute certainty.

Then, thinking the idea was totally dismissed, I continued on with my quest to find financial resources enough to keep my retreat centre buoyant from one month to the next.

This living month-to-month with barely anything ever leftover seemed too limited. Meanwhile, all the buildings begged for attention, and the costs involved with living in the rain forest on the West Coast of Canada ran high.

One day, I woke up, and one more contract didn't seem to do it for me any longer—in fact, I found myself dreading one more contract or one more person arriving at the centre.

I felt sick and tired of making ends meet and found myself asking for a new way; in short, a miracle. I wanted to find a way to sustain Xenia, taking the pressure off having to sell more beds. I was done with that game. It was far too much work. Instead, I wanted my freedom, and I wanted to help others in a more meaningful way. I was desperate to change course.

So, when the answer to this prayer arrived, disguised as relationship marketing, I dismissed it immediately. No way could this be my miracle. No way. Never. I rejected the person who'd offered this 'opportunity' to me. She asked for me to visit her in Portland and check it out. To which I replied, "Absolutely not; no way!!! "

Renee Beth had always impressed me in our earlier conversations about bringing leaders from around the world together to change the way we did education, business, and healthcare. So, it seemed a bit off-track that she was trying to recruit me into Network Marketing.

I had all kinds of judgments about why she would do such a thing; after all, she was a schoolteacher, executive coach, and more than qualified to do 'real' work, professional work. Renee Beth tried every angle to help me see what she could. I did notice how extremely committed to this thing she was, like a dog with a bone. After all, she'd driven over 500 kilometers to give me this "gift," as she put it.

"Angelyn, this is the dream you and I have had for years—to bring leaders from around the world together to build learning communities and help raise the consciousness of the planet. Don't you remember when we sat out on your porch with a bottle of red wine that day?" she said.

I did, but simply couldn't get myself fired up to hear what she had to say. In fact, as I sat in front of her, not listening to a word she uttered, I felt sorry for her. The inner critic came out in full force.

She phoned me six times in ten days and I couldn't believe her audacity. I kept repeating it was not for me. But, somehow, either she didn't listen to me, or she was the most tenacious person I had ever met.

Then, on Sunday evening, she phoned again. My body tensed up when I saw her number on my screen. I nearly didn't pick up the phone, but I felt sorry for her.

"Angelyn, before you say your final no, would you please download the audio clip I just sent you and listen to it. Please, will you do this for me? I'll never bother you again, I promise," she said.

My body let out a big sigh, and finally, I agreed.

It took 20 minutes to download the file, and then I reluctantly listened to what Renee Beth was so excited to share with me.

Within five minutes of listening to this rather inspiring interview with a brilliant scientist and top income earner in this company, something inside me opened up. He spoke of how a billionaire philanthropist, a Wall Street icon CEO, and he had agreed to do their highest and best. They placed their hands on top of each other as a gesture of commitment (like sharing blood).

Those three words got my attention—highest and best. Hearing this sparked a curiosity of truth. I had not yet achieved my highest and best, but in that moment, I knew I wanted to. I knew there was more, so much more, I came to planet earth to experience and deliver.

Despite my determination not to get sucked in, this concept of highest and best and the caliber of people involved stirred something in me, and I felt compelled to simply jump in with an investment I had no business making. I did not have the money but like always, if the intention is clear the money shows up. I borrowed it, promising to pay it back. Even though I was doubtful, something deep inside seemed so certain of this direction.

From that point on, I simply went to work and adapted this new venture into my amalgam, to see what I could co-create with a team of like-minded entrepreneurs.

My mentors taught me how to work with my strengths—strengths I didn't know I had and a whole new world opened up to me. In the beginning I thought I was going off track with my Calling but found out it was an important step along the way and very much part of and connected to my Calling.

In the first several months I absorbed as much as I could and showed up at everything. With my team I achieved success quickly and won bonuses for promotions I didn't even know about. By the end of the first month my business had moved through three ranks and I had not only recovered my initial investment, I doubled it.

Soon a wonderful tribe gathered around this mission. The momentum of the business carried me along a fast river of success. Sometimes we are guided to do things towards our deepest mission but don't always see how it relates. That was my problem in the beginning, but I found out quickly it was a game of transformation on every possible level and it served me well. I am now in my thirteenth year of great success and dedication with this business. I have won every award, including the highest award given by the company for servant leadership excellence and earned my first million dollars in the first three to four years. It literally saved Xenia from going back to the bank and now is fully integrated as a part of my life. It was and is aligned with my Calling.

When you think of your present job/career, if you have one, ask what percentage of you is showing up for work? What percentage of your skill and talent is being used every day? You may be surprised to find it is not very much. Sometimes a job or career may be totally part of the journey of your Calling and one day it is done and it's time to let it go. This is where I have found a lot of confusion and fear of letting go with my clients. How could it have been so important one minute and you pour your heart and soul into it and then it is over?

Sometimes it is not even about letting go of our career but instead realigning with what parts of the job we want to do and delegating the rest. Ultimately our Calling is not about a job, career, or any destination. It is the pathway upon which we travel and the thread that weaves through it.

JOURNAL WORK

So, the question is:

Are you ready to jump ship, have you already done so or do you need a bridge exit to your dream? Is it truly aligned with your Calling? Or are you needing to let go and move on?

**Disclaimer:** I am not encouraging you to simply quit your job without any financial support backing you. At the same time check and see if you have used money as an excuse and the reason why you have not taken the plunge yet. More about this in later chapters.

# CHAPTER FOUR

# What Makes Your Soul Sing?

*Let the beauty of what you love be what you do. —Rumi*

You are powerful beyond measure. Yet sometimes our beliefs get in the way and tell us we need a miracle to change direction. What you may consider a miracle or magic is in fact your birthright and not as mysterious as you may have been led to believe. The key is how to perceive it at these subtle and deep levels of insight.

## ASHING AND LISTENING

This is where the practice of meditation, silence, and prayer can point you in a direction to where you can find your answers. Through the portal of silence, you can unwrap a deeper picture of your soul.

Asking for what you want is not always the easiest thing to do but it is an important muscle to develop. When I lead workshops and ask people what they want, often the room goes quiet while they dig deep to come up with some answers. Most people do not honestly know. Many have never developed this muscle and the lifting of a dream is too much effort for them to bear.

Have you even gotten cynical and think, "Why bother? It's a waste of time!" Then you see others living their Calling and you feel a deep longing to be doing the same. Maybe you think, "He was given a hand up or born with a silver spoon in his mouth or maybe she is just lucky." I was told that so many times in my life and although I have worked very hard for my life today, I decided to agree. Yes, I'm lucky that I have faith in myself enough to ask for what I want and live my Calling now. The rest is about being willing to listen and risk taking action. To sometimes jump empty handed into the void. The art of discernment and adaptability are our teachers when you ask for what you want and, for most, this is a difficult process.

We have been so led to believe asking for what we want is a selfish act and I beg to differ. It's an important part of the equation and we can receive huge insight and abundance from doing so. Part of asking for what you want has to do with being willing to do what is then required of you to meet this outcome. Often this means taking risks and stepping out of the nine dots. Our conditioning has carved its pathways deep into our psyche.

When were you told on your way to school, "Have a great day and be sure to go out and take lots of risks…" ? No, we were told, "Be careful." Maybe your Calling is creative or as a healer but what kind of programming did you ever receive to support this when the usual message was about create money and that would come about by a particular job or career. Two completely different messages. So when we step out a little further, it may feel vulnerable and totally foreign to our system. This is good. This is growth.

The power of intention has a life force that creates outcome. It is like an arrow propelling towards its target unimpeded. On the other hand, attachment to this outcome repels and hinders its possibility. The art of having a strong outcome yet holding it gently, without attachment, is the secret to its success.

When I say my intention prayer and release it to the universe, I always ask that it be in the highest good of all.

I also have to be totally willing to let it go and know that if it doesn't manifest, that is perfect as well.

When I was giving a talk recently at a business breakfast, a lady came over to me afterwards and was telling me about her dream. She was clutching it so tightly there was no way it was free enough to manifest. It was static because of her hold on it. I gently said, "Okay, now can you let it go?" She looked at me in total amazement and horror. This was her baby; it was hard for her to imagine having trust enough to let it go.

I can understand this protection of the seed or idea, but this is where radical trust comes in and a willingness to know that you will actually survive if it doesn't happen. Are you more attached to the idea than wanting it to actually manifest? Because with every manifestation that occurs, your life changes. And to the degree of manifestation, so too, is the degree of change. Do you think my life changed when I manifested the Retreat Centre? Yes, just about every aspect of my life changed. So you have to be ready for change.

It's tricky sometimes to decipher whether you want the dream or you want 'to want' the dream. Is your hand raised or are you just talking about it again to folks willing to listen one more time to your story about what you are going to do one day in the future?

Another example, if you're wanting to manifest a close intimate relationship, this will mean big time change. Are you willing to make space for this change?

Some of my girlfriends have said to me, "I'm really ready for a relationship but for some reason I cannot attract anyone significant." I ask them how they feel about giving up some of their precious time for this to occur. At first they say, "Well yes, of course," but upon careful reflection realize that their calendars are totally booked or that they like their own space way too much.

The reason manifestations don't happen is usually related to one of three things:

- We're not connected to the source or it is not aligned with the Divine Plan.
- We really don't believe we deserve it.
- We're not willing to accept or manage our creation because of the change that will come about because of it.

I love manifestation and alchemy and watching how it works. It's quite easy now for me to see why I have blocked a manifestation and instead of being critical with myself I will just notice and investigate further how much I was really willing to make space for it. I do believe in the power of timing and alignment. There is a perfect order and serendipity to life and the more I surrender to it and have radical trust, the lighter and happier I feel.

I have learned to let go of many intentions I thought I wanted but really they were usually ego based requests which would not have been fulfilling anyway.

Everyone has an inner Calling, a core that is unique only to you. If you haven't already discovered this, now may be the time.

What is on your heart wanting expression? Maybe you already know what it is and it is just a matter of saying "Yes" and "Now."

Have you heard yourself saying you want to this and have that? Have you actually become really aware of what this is and how often you have said it and promised it to yourself? Or are you fast asleep at the wheel and totally unconscious of this going on in your head and heart for years? Have you promised to lose weight, to find the guy, to write a book, to travel the world, to change careers and do something more meaningful and closer to your heart? You noticed one year falls into the next and you are shocked by the way time is flying by. Before you know it another whole decade has passed you by and you still say these things you want but they haven't arrived yet.

Okay, let's break it down and find out why not. In this section we will do a deep dive to see if what you really do want is what you say you want.

In this very moment look around and know that everything you have in your life is exactly as you want it to be. Before you dismiss my comment, think about it. Take one aspect of your life and let's drill down on it. You will be amazed by what you discover.

## What do you really want?

Take one area—let's say regarding your new work, your soul work, your Calling. Write it down as specifically as you can. Tune in and sense whether it comes from your mind as a good idea or from a place deeper that feels more aligned with your heart and soul. There is a place deep within that calls to you and you only. It has a passionate flavour and special tone and you will know it by how happy it makes you feel. Sometimes we have to go to our childhood to seek places where we were in our bliss and there was no sense of time or space. You felt the buoyancy of life moving you and you knew all was well in your world. What were you doing and how were you doing it? It may not mean that is exactly what you want to be doing today but it is a clue and we are tracking it as information for our case.

As a child I loved horses; I was obsessed with them and I wanted to do whatever it took to be around them.

My dad said I left home at age six. I took to the woods. From an early age, I had this oneness with nature. I loved daydreaming in the woods or riding my pretend horse through the trails with my jam sandwiches and vast imagination.

Horses were my first real passion. I was crazy about them. For hours I would lay on my belly, drawing them in fine detail, learning all the names of the bones, muscles, and breeds. This hunger for horses was not shared by my parents, who didn't understand my fascination, much less afford it. I was relentless in my pleas for riding lessons; there had to be a way I could live in the domain of horses. Money was the condition my parents spoke of as the deciding factor. Coming from working-class with very young parents, it was not easy for them to provide for my dream. Since they couldn't afford to buy me a horse or pay for riding lessons, I showed my mum how I could be with horses.

For a living, she drove a small green van and in the back, she carried a variety of household products and clothing for children and mothers. She did well with her business, and people loved her. I pointed out some of her clients had horses, and there must be a way they would let me see them. To her credit, Mum made every attempt to get free rides for me from some of her customers, and this appeased me for a short while. This longing came from deep in my soul, and my determined spirit always jostled for ways to get out into the countryside where I could see and smell the horses.

When the obsession for horses took over, I tried every avenue possible to find a way to learn about them. Eventually a great connection was made with one of Mum's clients, where I was able to clean stables for free rides. Very quickly, I got established in the riding school, which lasted many years. Becky, the main instructor at the barn, became my mentor and taught me everything about horses. I used to ride my bike several miles to the riding stables, often in the dark, come rain or shine.

My bike was secondhand and, of course, in those days, didn't have gears, so the hills were daunting, but I never complained. I ended up working and living at the farm on weekends and throughout the long summer holidays. I would come home exhausted and smelling like horses but happy as could be.

One day, I bought a bucket in the hopes of getting a horse of my own. Not any old bucket, but a proper equestrian one from the local tack shop. I kept it in my bedroom for the day when I would realize my dream. I imagined my horse drinking from it in a beautiful pasture. The fantasies ran rampant in my head as I visualized owning and caring for my horse. At twelve years old, I was given "Regent" to take care of. He was an old, fine-looking white part-Arabian horse, in his mid-twenties. His owner had to go away and needed somebody to love him as their own for a year. What a great opportunity that was for me.

At sixteen, I procured Zargos, a four-year-old, stunning dappled grey Anglo-Arab. I had three jobs to repay the debt but didn't care because I had arrived in heaven.

Early one spring day, I went riding alone in the vast St. Leonard's Forest, which backed onto the stables. The sky shone blue, and the weather felt unseasonably warm for that time of year. Zargos felt alert and eager to go, and I could feel his excitement. Deep in the forest, on this powerful being, I became aware of the environment surrounding me in a way I had not experienced before.

I could literally hear the silence in the space between the birds singing and other beautiful sounds of nature. Over the lily of the valley, up the forest bank, and there in front of us was the two-mile chase. A wide-open dirt road, and I could feel the anticipation in Zargos as we prepared ourselves for a gallop.

Holding him back at first, I slowly released the reins. Then moving into full throttle, felt like zero to a hundred in moments. Before long, both of us were united, wild and free, racing against the shadows of ourselves. The sun surged down upon us, penetrating our bodies. The whole atmosphere and motion embraced me. Tears filled my eyes. There I flew, through the middle of the forest, not another person to be seen, galloping on this powerful beast and welling up with emotion for such beauty and happiness. I must have reached the utter climax of emotion—the gallop, an inconceivable feeling.

Until then, I had never experienced such a sensation of freedom as in those few magical moments. You may wonder why I share this story, but it really was part and parcel of the theme that would become my life's Calling. Not only horses, but the freedom and silence.

This space of oneness etched a pathway to my soul. It truly was a sweet spot where all the worries of the world stood still and utter peace and joy reigned. After that, I experienced it often, mostly when alone in nature. It became my little secret. I had no idea how this would follow throughout my whole life and take me to another country where I would realize my dream come true and yes, of course it included horses and nature and silence. *It was my Calling, calling to me.*

Take some time in nature to recall where you found your bliss as a child and take notes.

Sometimes what you want isn't always clear, especially if you have several talents.

I thought my daughter was going to be a businesswoman and get her MBA, based on her love for creating and selling things as a child. Being my daughter, she was exposed to horses and loved them as I did. Her business ventures were for the sole purpose of buying her own horse. One day she asked me to pick up 200 plain candles for her because she wanted to paint them, package them, and sell them at the Christmas Craft fair.

At first I didn't take her seriously, until she reminded me of her bid. She reiterated her request for 200 candles and if I could get them at the best price possible, so she could make a profit. Setting up a little workspace in one of the cabins, she went about creating the most beautiful paint-dipped candles. The packaging was just as lovely with cedar clippings, sparkles and ribbons embellishing the little gifts. Her confidence was strong, yet vulnerable, as she sold every last one of them at the Craft Fair.

When she tallied up her expenses and paid back her investor (me) and paid for the table, she earned $325 in profit. She was eight years old. Other times she sold herbs from the garden or hand painted stones. I was sure she was going to be a businesswoman, an entrepreneur. All the while, her drive came from wanting to buy her horse.

Then surprise of all surprises, she took up part-time work at our local vet clinic. I didn't think she would be able to survive, given her squeamish nature around the sight of blood.

A few years of working in the clinic after school and during school holidays in combination with her love for horses, and her soul led her to her vocational Calling. She is now an Equine Veterinarian specializing in sports medicine. She simply loves it and boy, did she work hard to get to where she is today. She learned chiropractic care for horses and rehabilitation. She will never stop learning and is basically on her path. And of course, she has two beautiful horses of her own.

If I track how she came to her work, it had everything to do with her Calling. She has a profound sweetness with people and a ferocious love for horses. Even though she had a thing about blood and operations and things she saw on TV as a child, she outgrew that phase and clearly is honouring her Calling.

As a parent we never really know where our children will end up in their careers and I think it's important to let them lead from their own knowing. I had a friend who loved horses and really wanted her daughter to love them as well.

However, growing up, the daughter had zero interest in them and ended up being an accountant. We just don't know what is right for our children but if we pay very close attention, they will give us clues. I hope these examples gave you ideas about what you want to do now. Did you relate to any part of my story? What has been nagging you? What have you not finished or accomplished yet?

# How long have you wanted this dream?

How long have you been thinking about this? I had a vision that followed me around for nine years before it manifested. It wasn't something my mind wanted or I thought was a good idea. It wasn't even something I had experience with, but it was within me awaiting expression. This dream arose from deep within as an urge or longing with a vision of what it would look like and feel like. In this vision I saw a beautiful 40-acre sanctuary in nature with meadows, trees, swings, and animals. Along with the vision, I received an inspired message that it was for the magical child within all, to feel safe to be creative. Pretty clear, hey? My Calling was drawing me in.

How long have you felt a longing to create something or contribute something? Maybe you pushed it down because it didn't happen in a year or two. If you sit quietly, you may feel it stirring once again like a bear waking up out of its hibernation. Each one of us has, locked deep within the crevices of our soul, an important gift. A seed containing a holographic component of truth. This seed comes tattooed to us at birth - it is our birthright.

We are all given certain gifts or better to say, we have earned specific gifts that are pertinent to our soul's evolution and our human journey in this lifetime. These gifts, like a loyal dog, are always there for us to use and no matter how we ignore, abuse, or throw them away, they will continue to return and look up at us with tenacious enthusiasm.

## Why do you want it?

'Why' is a very important question to ask yourself. It is the deepest part of you that drives the aspiration. When you know your 'why,' the filter is clear. There is only one option and you know what it is. Check out Simon Sinek's TED Talk on You Tube about starting with your WHY. It is so well done that I wanted to make mention of it here.

I've noticed with myself and my clients that our WHY isn't always obvious at first and although Sinek advocates it should be the first place you look while setting up a business venture, I have found sometimes you back into your WHY. In other words, you follow an instinct or vision and you don't exactly know why in the beginning but you are drawn into following it. It could be a year or two into the project before you start to uncover your "why." That happened for me in my relationship marketing business. I thought my why was about the money I needed and it wasn't until a year or two later I discovered my real "why" and mostly, why I had been drawn into this industry. It was all about transformation and witnessing this taking place in the people I was working with. It was totally aligned with my true Calling.

## How will you feel if this dream never happens?

This is the true "come to Jesus" moment. Facing the thought of 'if it didn't happen,' you will either feel relief and you can let it go or you will feel deep sadness for not having given it your all. For not risking and challenging yourself with it. You may feel devastated at the thought.

By investigating this question, you will get the truth of whether you want to follow this deeper path and if you are ready to.

There is a difference between being unattached and unintended. It is a very important distinction to make.

Once you get clear about this, you can do some internal housecleaning and purge yourself of the stories and things you are spending time thinking you want to achieve and will do 'one day' when you know already you will not. This opens up space for you to connect with what you do want and what your heart and soul are really calling for.

## What has not honouring your Calling cost you?

Tell yourself the truth about what not doing this or giving this to yourself has cost you. What price have you paid for your resistance? Maybe you have paid a very high price including your health. Perhaps you have become apathetic and dispirited.

This is not living. This is existing as an empty shell. Postponing your joy for the future is a problem I see often, and it wreaks havoc with the soul who wants to emerge now.

Some of my clients used their weight as a reason to hide behind their own power and ability. Some felt overweight and others underweight. They referred to this as to why their life wasn't working out. If this has happened to you and you think the weight is the problem, it is not. It goes far deeper than that to an original wound that has not yet been met with understanding. Look for a time when you experienced an energy break because you were damaged at your core and you hid your essence. This is where you will discover your answers.

Are you using the "weight" story as your excuse to "wait" and not show up fully? You may tell yourself, "When I lose weight, I will show up." The problem with this is it creates enormous separation and disconnects you from the very thing you want, which is to make a difference and be who you really are now. Not sometime in the future when all the stars align.

It is far too easy to succumb to complacency and live in avoidance when you fall into the trance of the mind. Filling your days with meaningless activities like Netflix and social media, are ways of eating up time and avoiding having to show up.

And the biggest thief of all is staying in a job long after you have outgrown it.

In the next chapters we will look at how to open pathways of awareness (OPA), so you don't just have information, instead you have awareness. It is in the awareness that change is possible.

CLARIFYING

### What are you willing to do, be or give up for this dream? How big is your impulse to act?

Your impulse to act has to be stronger than your resistance. You may not yet have stepped forward for one of many different reasons. Here are a few, I'm sure you can find many more:

Money, time, ability, courage, support, other commitments, confidence, confusion, worthiness.

We will look deeper at these aspects in later chapters but for now make a note of any areas that resonate when you ask yourself the questions:

- What are the excuses your mind is throwing up about why it hasn't happened yet?
- What has been standing in your way?

- How will you feel when you are living your Calling?

*A bird is safe in its nest but that is not what its wings are made for."* — *Amit Ray*

Something profound kicks in when we're inspired from within, rather than motivated by an external goal or person. When we feel the intrinsic power of inspiration and sense that our life depends on it, we feel the urgency. If we are obligated to someone else's agenda, our life force is drained. When we are working in our Calling, we conjure up fuel seemingly out of thin air to ignite our engine and we find ourselves revved up in a way we have never experienced before.

Visualize yourself if you can, living the dream and honouring your Calling right now. What exactly are you doing and how exactly does it feel? If you cannot see this as a reality in your mind's eye perhaps this is not what you really want after all. We will be getting to levels and layers of letting go so as to free up space for what you really want.

- What emotionally moves you when your work has been effective? What is stirred in others?
- When your work has been effective, what have you proved to yourself about yourself?
- If you have no choice but to create (choose one thing) what would you create?

  When I was first asked this question way back in the 80s, I said:

  *I would create revolutionary changes in thinking and attitudes in the people in decision-making positions. That's everyone.*

  When I look at that now nearly 40 years later, I see the seed that was planted and I'm sure it went back even further from my fascination with transformation and why some people succeeded at things and others didn't and why some people had more courage than others.

JOURNAL WORK

Do a meditation and visualize what your life would be like living your Calling. If you would like help, please check out the meditation I have created on my website: angelyntoth.com/meditation.

When I set an intention, I usually put it down on paper. Hand writing it in the present tense. There is a power when we write down our power packed words on paper and it sends a message to the universe of our intention. Here is an example:

### Yes...Congratulations!

I   (name)   am so grateful now that

_____(fill in the blank) _____

_____

_____(signature)   (date)_____

# CHAPTER FIVE

# What Stops You?

Sometimes you don't know you are stopped, and in this chapter, we will look at ways of knowing if this is true. Or is it simply timing and not being aware of what the possibilities are? We will look at three important areas that help us see clearly, trust radically, and amp up our optimism levels to pull off what may feel like a near impossible feat.

**Our world is our mirror.**

If you are unsure of what is going on inside of yourself, look around at your world and see the mirrors reflected back at you. I was working with a client recently and she was going on about all the flakey people she was surrounded by. She cited the reason her business wasn't growing was because of these flakey people. I asked her if she could find flakiness inside herself. She responded immediately with "No way, I always make my appointments and do what I say I'm going to do." She felt a little unhinged by my questioning. I asked again, "Is there anywhere in your life you can find where you are being flakey?" No response. She couldn't find it. Then I asked her, "What about with yourself?"

She took a moment to consider this question and that is when the penny dropped and tears filled her eyes. She found how flakey she had been with herself. Making promises to herself and never keeping them. It was a profound realization and with this awareness she was able to make a change.

Without awareness you can never make a change. I've heard the saying you cannot change what you do not acknowledge. It is even deeper than that. I know a person who has all the knowledge about her situation and what she wants. She is a very bright lady, astute and clear. She has all the words to explain the situation and even counsels other people on the subject. But she doesn't have the results herself.

Her language always places her results in the future. Years and years pass by and still the plan is in the future. She has the information but doesn't have the awareness. If suddenly she has the awareness, it would happen at lightning speed or she would release the plan she thought she wanted.

Once you start to become aware of what thoughts and stories are running the show, stay open to the way life moves you and offers you all kinds of help all the time. Asking for and receiving help may be something you could get way better at and my hope is this may prompt you into the habit of asking.

Another reason you may be stopped from having what you want is because clearly you haven't been ignited from your deepest core. I call this lighting your inner candle.

### Lighting the Candle as a True Witness

We all need to be witnessed to fully emerge into our Calling. According to Maslow's Hierarchy of Needs [2] this doesn't happen until our basic physiological and psychological needs are met. This

---

[2] McLeod, S. A. (2017). Maslow's hierarchy of needs. Retrieved from www.simplypsychology.org/maslow.htm

would include food, shelter, water, safety, belonging, love, etc. Self-actualization is seen as a final step towards this total fulfillment stage and can only occur after our basic needs are met. True witnessing is like lighting an inner candle and letting yourself be seen as you truly are in each moment. This is where our Calling lives. And even after a full career, you still may feel unseen at your deepest level because you still haven't offered the gift you were born to deliver. The Calling is your gift, your alignment, your soul, your oneness with all that is.

My theory is we each come into life with an unlit inner candle, and to activate it, you need to be witnessed in the purest sense by another person. Our parents and teachers would make the likeliest candidates, but usually, this doesn't get the job done. There are many 50 and 60+ year old's who still have not felt fully witnessed. In our society we get praised and punished, not just for who we are, but for our character and what we achieve and do for a living. So, when a person comes along and sees us, at the core, it sparks an awakening and unlocks us to our Calling. And from there, it can produce exponential growth. "When two or more are gathered..." so to speak.

Many live out their whole lives without ever feeling seen, or having their candle lit. And without this bonding, they may feel separate and unable to fulfill their soul's longing. This often precipitates a feeling of loss and a person acts needy because they never got the right attention. They're always looking for attention but never actually receiving it. Have you been looking for this attention in all the wrong places?

The distinction of being seen, not from a behavioral point of view or from your pedigree, assets or, for that matter, liabilities, but from the deepest place within where the dwelling of consciousness arises. To touch this place is the sweet spot, the place of connectedness, and here the join up occurs, and the candle gets lit.

This is not to be confused with needing other people to acknowledge you as in the insatiable appetite of the ego, but if just once you are seen at the core of your being, you can carry the flame from that point forth.

If you want to light someone's candle, listen, really listen to his or her story. Listen with presence, not with judgment, or with sympathy or trying to fix them, or with trying to save them.

Everyone has a story they need to share, and in this sharing, if done with presence, the story gets met with understanding. And in the truest sense it is listening way beyond the story into the essence of who they are.

After you have been witnessed (ignited), you can pay it forward. Being present and in your essence is the key to being able to witness another. Holding a neutral space without judgment because now you can hear yourself, gives space for intelligence to come through.

Have you noticed during an argument how there is back and forth with each person trying to be heard and holding their ground on an issue? The other retaliates with their comeback and the unconscious communication bounces around but never really lands. If one person stopped, became present, and brought their full awareness into their heart, the other person would be able to actually hear themselves. This is how we witness each other.

Not until I reached my thirties did I ever feel witnessed in this unconditional and non-judgmental way. Where I felt seen, not just from my persona but from the core of my Being. Chrystalle was my first true witness and devoted friend. She saw my Calling as clear as a bell and way before I fully understood it. It turned out we were each other's first real witness.

She told me she was invisible until she met me. I feel fortunate and blessed to have had her in my life and, for sure, I aligned with my Calling as a result of her seeing me.

When we first met, it was no ordinary meeting where two friends had a lot in common. It was two opposites with a shared mission. Certain Angels get assigned to us for specific purposes and she is one such Earth Angel. Chrystalle felt the same way about me witnessing her. Here's how she explained it:

## Meeting Angelyn

*For the first thirty-eight years of my life, I lived in the 'Wilderness,' relatively speaking. I spent my time observing life and its processes removed from participating in life. No*

*people existed in my life. Not knowing any other way, I didn't*
*realise fully how lonely an existence this was.*
*I went on with my self-directed studies in how things worked*
*through reading how-to books. The other topic that grabbed*
*my interest came from biographies—my contact with people.*
*Then, one day, I met a Guardian Angel in an office in the*
*middle of downtown Vancouver. At first, I didn't recognize*
*the water offered to me in my desert but meeting Angelyn was*
*the beginning of my metamorphosis.*

*-written by Chrystalle in 1998*

My life has changed radically since Chrystalle lit my inner candle. Something came awake in me that I had not experienced at that level before. I felt a quiet confidence in myself and this gave me all kinds of permission to do the things I really wanted to do. Chrystalle was my comrade and best friend for 25 years and we accomplished so much together, including the first 12 years of building Xenia, my retreat centre. When she died at the age of 61 it seemed far too early and it was hard to get over this loss in the beginning. She was my best friend and my daughter's godmother.

Her spirit carried on and I was shown just how thin this veil really is. I also learned that once this candle has been lit, it continues to shine brightly even when Chrystalle was no longer physically present in my life. I feel her presence often just like the Angel she was on earth.

As a practice at the retreat centre, we started doing Gratitude Circles for people's birthdays and giving them words of appreciation with loving kindness. By the time we got to the last few people they were usually filled to the brim with loving emotion and some having a hard time receiving. But we all got better at it. The comments had to be heartfelt and genuine, no nicey-nice stuff for the sake of it.

After that, I became committed to Gratitude Circles in my work at Xenia and while some people squirmed in their seats, they admitted afterwards it was beautiful. I love hosting these circles. It is like giving someone an emotional massage. And everyone deserves a good listening to and acknowledgement.

Have you ever felt seen for your gift at your core and the deepest parts of your soul? Have you ever felt like a person really gets you?

Some people were fortunate to have been witnessed growing up, while at the same time being able to receive it. I bet it had a very big impact on them. I say receive it because sometimes as much as a very present, caring person coming from essence tries to witness another, it doesn't always ignite. It may not be the time, or the way. When it does happen this bonding creates safety and grounds us to the world.

I have observed many people with something missing in their eyes and I can tell they have never really been seen. It is too vulnerable for them to let this connection in. A big part of our work at the centre is witnessing them as they are at their core. I do my best whenever possible to see them at this very special place if they are open to receiving. It is the most important thing we can offer to another and that is our full attention and awareness. This has the highest possibility of igniting their inner flame.

## Radical Trust

One of the biggest reasons you may be stopped from honouring your Calling and taking steps into the unknown, even when your heart and soul knows what to do, is a lack of trust. Following an invisible light through the dark woods is not for the faint of heart, but it is exactly what is being called forth. Will you be supported; will you know what to do? And ultimately can you trust life itself and God, Spirit, the Divine or whatever term you use for this almighty power? In many ways I don't think we really trust until we have been tested and brought to our knees in surrender. I wish it could be easier, but for me it was a total surrender and death of a kind. I discovered radical trust, not as a concept but as a direct experience that eventually led me to my life's work.

As I mentioned earlier I had this vision that followed me around for nine years, of a beautiful 40+ acre retreat centre in nature with horses and meadows and lakes. I understood it was for the magical child within all to feel safe to be creative. Without the funds to realize this dream, I kept dismissing it from my mind.

Soon I was to learn, *you don't have a vision, a vision has you.* And you're not given a vision without the resources to make it happen, though they're probably not handed to you on a silver platter. I'm in awe of the complexity of weaving that goes on within the universe to unfold such a vision and synchronize absolute growth and change at the same time if one is ready.

At what turned out to be a pivotal point in my life, I was asked to do something that made no sense to me at all, something I had no interest in. Period. I was repeatedly nudged by a deep whisper inside to go back to my distanced husband.

No way, I thought, and dismissed this as a ridiculous idea. Eventually the inner stirring was so insistent that I had to consider it until finally and reluctantly, I obeyed the message. The journey of sewing together a broken relationship was difficult and really made no sense. It was painful and ripped at my soul because I didn't understand why I had been asked to go back. I will spare you all the details and reasons why I shouldn't have gone back except to say it involved the safety of my four-year-old daughter and myself.

Worn down by this inner stirring, I eventually went back but as I suspected, it wasn't good and the same problems were still happening. What was I thinking!?

Three months later, in despair, I received a further message from this place deep within, that I could let go again. WHAT, let go of what? "The marriage," came the response. I was flabbergasted. What did all this mean? I would have to uproot my daughter once more and lose the respect of my friends and family who hadn't thought it was a good idea in the first place. It felt a little crazy to put it mildly, but I followed this insane instruction from this deep place within and let go of my marriage one more time. My belief in my inner listening was dwindling and because it was such a strong part of me, I felt vulnerable and kind of abandoned in some way.

One year later, my husband died suddenly from heart failure. He was 41 years old. It was a devastating shock and an unbelievable task to console our five-year-old daughter, who did not understand. My own grief was bad enough but when the grief of my child was added, it became unbearable.

Unbeknownst to me I received a very large inheritance, one I was not in any way expecting since we had already separated our assets. It was a great deal of money, enough to secure the property in the vision that followed me around.

The significant piece here is: lawyers informed me that if I hadn't been back with my husband for three months, the insurance company and the courts would have had the right to treat our split as a de facto divorce, resulting in a much lower disbursement. The consequence of this proved enormous, as this inheritance provided me with more money than I had ever known before and enough to begin a lifelong dream.

Huge emotions prevailed. I had to reconcile the thoughts, feelings, and judgments from his family. I didn't want my husband to die for my vision but here it was. This is what reality served up and if I hadn't listened to this deep instruction from within, this vision never would have happened. Some may call it coincidence but for me it was the awakening of radical trust.

Now 26 years later and having manifested this retreat centre called Xenia Creative Development Centre, I can feel how much it was meant to be and how guided the process has been and continues to be. Thousands of people's lives have been helped by the programs offered here and by the energy in the land itself. Dorothy Maclean, co-founder of Findhorn in Scotland (one of the largest retreat centres in the world), visited and connected with the elemental kingdom, saying this place was chosen a long time ago and has an ordained role. Eckhart Tolle and other great people have visited Xenia. We are blessed.

Sometimes I think about how my life would have been different without this radical trust. I now live in implicit faith of the divine plan, and it always blows me away how big and awesome that plan is. Radical trust is 100% commitment, and nothing less. 99% will not do and therein lies the question.

- o  Do you trust completely that you are safe and there is a beautiful plan for you?
- o  Do you trust that you matter so much you cannot even fathom how much?

- Do you know what you have to say and express is so important?
- Is your heart calling you to show up and be of service in a new way?

You may already feel like you have done your best work and achieved some amazing feats yourself. Maybe you want to enjoy your second or third act in a quieter way. And yes, good luck with that. My experience is that it just amps up whenever we ask the question "How may I be of service?"

I asked that very question two years after my husband died, sitting on a boardwalk on the lake that actually backed onto the land that (unbeknownst to me) I was going to purchase. Friends encouraged me to retire early and live off my inheritance. They said I could relax and sip wine on my balcony overlooking the ocean all day long. The thought crossed my mind as a wonderful idea for five minutes but soon I was feeling the urge from my soul to contribute and show up. I still wasn't able to fully surrender to my true Calling because it felt so selfish and I believed I was supposed to do something more traditional and "normal." Plus, it was hard to reconcile that my husband's death was what provided the funds for this to happen. I struggled for quite some time, feeling responsible and hesitant to put money into the dream I knew was aligned with my heart and soul. Instead, I put the money into other investments Financial Advisers told me to. After all they were the experts and I was not. Unfortunately this didn't pan out well and I'll share more about this later.

My beloved vision sat on the back burner for two more years and here again I trust the divine guidance that waits patiently for us to wake up. So, when you ask "How may I be of service?", expect to get an answer that comes with it and the means to make it happen.

Our programming and conditioning are often so dense that we're not even aware of the rules we have bought into. Or the limitations that we have accepted as true when in fact they are not. We have so much ability at whatever age to create and manifest our dreams and always, there has to be a way. I have never been very good at taking 'no' for an answer, especially when I can see it in my mind's

eye.   As we get older don't we get even bolder?
Sometimes being outrageous is perfectly okay and
necessary to accomplish our deepest passion.  And if
not now, when?

### Radical Trust

*There is so much wisdom held within the flame*
*Into which the moth surrenders its life*
*Not from wisdom but from instinct*
*It has no choice*
*It cannot resist the attraction*
*Any more than you can*
*And the more you turn away*
*The more pain will surface*
*Be not afraid of such strong waves of pull*
*And with all the vigour of*
*The child leaping into water*
*Throw yourself in and know the Truth*
***You were thrown***

*—Angelyn*

# CHAPTER SIX

## Unreasonable Optimism

As unrelated as this next story seems, I wanted to share it to demonstrate how important it is to ask for what we want and need. And to emphasize that when it presents itself, how important it is to be able to receive it. If I didn't have the unreasonable optimism I have, many, many things wouldn't have happened. But to illustrate my point, I'd like to share this story:

It was the day after New Year's and I was taking a young friend and my daughter to the movies. It happened to be at the mall where my daughter's orthodontics office was.

Driving over towards the mall, she informed me of her sore mouth. At a traffic light I looked into her mouth and saw a horrible looking groove in her gum from the protruding wire.

"That must hurt!" I exclaimed.

"Yes Mum, it's killing me."

"Well let's go see if Dr. Jones is in her office today."
Of course we all looked at each other with the thought, Yeah right…not today. No dentist office will be open during the Christmas and New Year's holidays. But onwards we went.

Making our way along the narrow corridor of darkened offices we saw that yes, just as we had suspected, the offices were all closed for the holidays. We almost turned around before reaching the doorway at the far end, but we kept going even though it seemed crazy. I just felt the pain my daughter was in and wanted a miracle to happen for her.

With *unreasonable optimism*, I tried opening the door and sure enough, it was locked.

We stood for a moment as if stuck there, when I saw someone in the side window. I peeked in and to my astonishment it was Dr. Jones herself with a watering can in her hand. She was in there watering the plants. At first, I tapped gently on the window to get her attention, but she didn't hear me and proceeded to go to the sink for water for the plants.

My daughter was pulling at my arm. "Mum, don't. Stop it. She's on holiday...let's go quick...come let's go..." She was embarrassed.

I nearly agreed with her and walked away, but I asked her how sore her mouth was. She said, "Very...but Mum, it can wait, it's okay."

I found myself knocking one more time on the window and suddenly the doctor caught sight of me and I waved.

She put her watering can down, came over right away with a smile on her face and unlocked the door.

"Hello, Happy New Year! What are you guys doing here from Bowen Island?"

I said, "I'm sorry to bother you, but my daughter's mouth is so sore. We happened to be in the area and took the chance to see if you were open today." I motioned for Kasara to show her.

"Oh please come on in...it's so great that you caught me." She motioned for us to follow her to her station and she mentioned that it was quite a coincidence she had come in to water the poinsettias since the offices would be closed for a week.

Looking into my daughter's mouth and seeing the inflamed gums from the rubbing of the braces, she said: "I can see how sore this must have been, I'm so glad you came in."
She happily took care of the problem and we were all so grateful.

Making our way down the corridor my daughter said: "Wow, Mum what are the chances of her being there at that exact moment?"
I said, "Yes babe, and when miracles like that happen, we have to make sure we receive them."
"Yes," she said with such relief in her voice. "We nearly walked away."

Now that was pure unreasonable optimism. I can think of many times I felt this open spaciousness inside and set about something that was utterly ridiculous.

One time I couldn't get a mortgage renewal because of bad credit ratings, but I found a way to reach out to the CEO of the credit union and pleaded my case. And voilà, I got the mortgage and at an excellent rate.

Another time I phoned a lawyer on a Sunday at his downtown office. When he picked up, he said, "Why would you think to call me here on a Sunday?" I said, "Because I needed to talk to you." Of course this was way before everyone carried a cell phone.

When I read The Power of Now, I knew I wanted to meet Eckhart so I found a way through a friend of a friend. Before long we were having brunch in Vancouver and later he came and spent the day with me at my retreat centre. People asked me how that happened, and I simply said: I asked. I do have unreasonable optimism and for the most part it works if it is sincere and in alignment. And I never take this for granted.

If you are willing to ask for what you want and do what is needed, you will see very quickly if it is aligned for you by the results you get. Are you consistent about asking for what you want? Yes, you will have to stretch beyond your present status and there are tools to help you with this. If you hesitate and hold back, life could pass you by. Every one of us has something unique and very important to offer in this lifetime. Do you have the courage now to deliver this and if not now when?

You never have to accept the status quo or let others stop you. Instead, you need to get even more unreasonable. Have fun with it and see what happens. As you get older, have you noticed how, not only do you get bolder, you start to relax about caring what people think of you? Screw what they think! When I look back, I remember how other people's opinion immobilized me at times and I held myself back for years before having the courage to proceed. Boy, getting over that one thing was truly liberating.

Who gives a shit anyway? Nobody really cares about what you do. And if they do and if they have judgments, that's on them, not you. Have empathy for them because they don't know the truth and feel separate from you. Miracles are being offered to you all the time and often you are unaware of them or leave just before they are about to happen. Tune in and stay present after you make a request. Trust that it will be delivered.

Can you remember a time when this happened for you already? I'm sure you can. Once you find it you have the road map. I vividly remember a friend of mine stating she wanted to find a beautiful cottage to rent by my retreat centre and she was only willing to pay $500 a month for it. Now that was total *unreasonable optimism* in that particular real estate market.

Guess what, exactly what she was asking for became available and it was worth at least triple the rent. But she got a fabulous cottage in a four-acre heavenly property for $500. It was a total surprise but her decision and commitment to it was certain. She visualized it into reality and held it there without wavering until it appeared. She knows the roadmap for this kind of manifestation, even though she doesn't always remember to use it.

Where does this power of inspiration come from and how can we bottle it and sell it?

That's my muse and challenge.

To imagine living your Calling may be out of the question. So might doing the kind of job you want to do or mission you would like to fulfill. It may take unreasonable optimism to get it started and it doesn't always work out, but when it is aligned, it has to happen.

I love the show Million Dollar Genius where ordinary people have a light bulb moment and come up with an invention or solution to a problem. Not only do they get the idea, but most of them are inspired to create it in prototype form before bringing in to investors. To me, this is the spirit of unreasonable optimism I'm talking about. Ask yourself if you are satisfied within your soul. Are you fully at peace with your expression thus far? I would bet you will not feel quenched until you have achieved what you came here to do.

What is your contribution?

What is your legacy?

Your deepest dream for your life may be a silent whisper deep in the crevices of your soul, yet to be known.

Are you hiding your essence from the world? There is some intelligence in shielding yourself from outside judgment and criticism, but this creates barriers and we are unable to receive, grow, or learn.

The only way out is to open up our hearts again. When you become present and move into your heart you see there is no need to protect your essence. You can let your guard down and shine your light brightly.

In theory you can imagine being a receiving tower, but you have a tight metal lid on top that cannot be penetrated. That is what it is like. So, learning how to open and stay open is a very important part of our work.

JOURNAL WORK

Where do you relate to this level of action and commitment? Write down choices you have made that have hindered your progress and any fears that were created. Note thoughts and feelings that go along with any excuses you hear. Be very gentle and compassionate with yourself as you identify these stories and excuses. This exercise is to bring awareness to what may be stopping you from having the life you deserve. No need to analyze this too much. Just keep opening to whatever is arising as a result of asking these questions. (More about this in Chapter 6).

SECTION TWO

# Pathways

In the second section of this book I share pathways with you to learn a process that helps you climb up a ladder of competency and bring awareness to any overwhelm that may be blocking your path. You will learn how to shift it and move up a ladder to the space of the Enthusiast where you unlock your capacity to honour your Calling.

There are many ways to reach for your dreams and tap into your Calling. It's important to find your unique way that resonates and opens you up to new possibilities.

In this Pathways section, my wish is for you to find a pathway that supports you in taking steps to arrive at the trailhead of your Calling

In the next chapter you will find three very specific ways in which my clients and I have experienced profound results towards this end.

# CHAPTER SEVEN

# Three Powerful Tools for Transformation

## *Beliefs*

B eliefs are thoughts we keep having and agree with, albeit unconsciously most of the time.

Beliefs run our lives and we move forward or hold back based on what we believe. Since every belief is derived from the past, you could say they are outdated the moment they form. A pure moment is met without any belief – open and aware to all that is arising in the present moment.

Beliefs can play havoc with us whether we know what they are, or whether they are running in the unconscious underground. Bringing awareness to them is important if they are holding us back. Getting free to do the work we want to do in the world with our passion and accumulated knowledge and skills can be arrested by a belief we have about ourselves or others. Questioning beliefs that no longer serve us is a great practice. In a sense we are taking them out of the unconscious 'Yes' into the conscious "No" by our awareness of them. Exposing beliefs can certainly take time, but as we become more and more aware of what they are, we can release them with love for the job they have done for us up until now. Sometimes we can overcome them by taking huge action in a different direction and other times we have to do the work.

I love all the movies that portray massive transformation where a person had to find the courage to act in a completely different way. Where they had to stretch beyond their comfort zone and find success. Recently I watched The Dawn Wall where legendary free climber Tommy Caldwell tries to get over a heartbreak by scaling 3000 ft of an impossible rock face. It's a documentary well worth watching.

As you get older you may not have this kind of ambition or stamina to create big dreams. Yet if there is still a niggling feeling inside asking you to reach forward into a new direction, you would be served greatly by listening to that. I've heard it said many times that you are not given more than you can handle even if it is a stretch. I have also had a sign on my fridge for years that says: You are never given a dream without the power to make it come true. The distinction here is being given – it is an intrinsic thing, not an external idea. Any form of inner stirring is saying yes...*Yes & Now*.

Many years ago, I went through a dark night of the soul experience precipitated by losing $350,000 in what turned out to be a fraudulent mortgage investment trust. I had a belief running that I had caused this dark night of the soul because I signed a document that I clearly shouldn't have signed. My mind was screaming, "NO. DON'T SIGN IT." I hadn't listened. In spite of the red flashing lights, and anxiety swelling in my belly, I buried my head in the sand and signed the document anyway. I felt powerless and uninformed.

Ever since then my mind ran a continuous story: You shouldn't have signed that document. Why didn't you listen? You idiot! This inner critic wouldn't let up until I became present to it one day waiting in the ferry line on my way to another lawyers' meeting. I was in the process of suing a bank manager who was found to be in cahoots with the financial adviser who sold me the investment, and they were attempting to get me to settle. The stress of working with lawyers and sorting this mess out felt awful, and I wanted to get free of the whole thing. I knew I was a victim of a fraudulent investment, but I felt responsible for my part by being attracted to it in the first place and not saying no.

Sitting in my car in the ferry line-up and hearing this crap from my mind, I phoned my friend Wendy to catch up, but honestly, more for a person to connect with regarding my dilemma. I was telling her how hard I was on myself for having signed the contract when I shouldn't have. She said not to go on the ferry. Instead, she said, go home and she would send me some questions I needed to answer. She said I would find peace from it.

I went home, and Wendy introduced me to the work of Byron Katie[3]. She told me to download a worksheet, fill it in, and then phone her back. She asked me the following questions:

W: So, you shouldn't have signed the papers, is that true?

A: No, I shouldn't have; I had a bad feeling about it.

W: Can you, absolutely, know for sure you shouldn't have signed it when you did?

A: Well I still think I shouldn't have. It was a big mistake.

W: Did you sign it?

A: Yes, I did.

W: How do you react every time you tell yourself the story that you shouldn't have signed it when you did?

A: I berate myself. I tell myself I'm stupid. I'm mad at myself. I cannot forgive myself for not listening to my gut screaming 'NO'. I was an idiot to get scammed.

---

[3] http://thework.com/en/do-work

W: Who would you be if you could never believe the thought again: "You shouldn't have signed the document when you did?"

After a pause, I could feel the tension leaving my body. I got it right away.

A: I would be free.

I could see that it did happen and I could do nothing about it now. It was done, and that was that. Almost right away, I was filled with acceptance about what happened. I forgave myself in that moment and haven't looked back.

I realized what happened actually brought many gifts, and it led me to the great work of Byron Katie and much more transformation. It was a $350,000 lesson, and I would not let it affect me one more minute. Struggling with reality was insane, and I had now become sane.

I later attended a nine-day school for the work of Byron Katie in California. It was life-changing and it's ridiculous how simple, yet potent the four questions and turnarounds are. I highly recommend you check it out.

If you recognize any particular belief that you have been holding onto, maybe now is the time to inquire into the validity of it today. Sometimes beliefs are so outdated and fearful, we have long moved on but forgotten to update our belief filing system. I recommend going back to earlier chapters and answering some of the questions to see if there is a subtle belief standing in the way.

## *Instinctive Patterns*

It is said, when the student is ready the teacher will appear, and this is when I met Elinor Meney. She is a Peak Performance Coach for Instinx[4] and licensed teacher of other coaches. We connected when I was on a trip to Australia, which is where she was living at the time. Being a ravenous student of transformation, I adopted this very potent tool and started working with her right away. I learned our instincts go even deeper than our beliefs. In most cases these instincts are formed at birth and during the earlier developmental years. How do you access

---

[4] Elinor Meney www.schoolofinstinx.com

them? How do you know what they are? How do you change them? Can you change them?

Elinor, born in British Columbia, had moved to Australia with her husband when her two daughters were quite young. Shortly after I met her, she decided to return to BC to be close to her aging parents.

One day, while chatting with Elinor by Skype while she was in Australia, she said, "Oh, by the way, I had a dream a few months ago I wanted to share with you."

"You and I", she continued, "were driving down a steep mountain" and before she could get out her next sentence, I stopped her. It triggered a dream I'd had a few months earlier, one that impacted me so much it stayed with me for days. I wrote it down and kept meaning to tell Elinor but forgot until I heard her say those few opening words.

I asked if, instead of her telling me, I could share the story to see if it was the same. She agreed, and I carried on the narrative, "Yes, we drove down this steep mountain. I sat in the driver's seat and you were in the passenger seat. I caught a glimpse of a powerful view coming up on the left, way below us. The road ran so narrow and steep I didn't dare take my eyes off it. Understanding the situation, you said to me, 'I'll hold the wheel, while you take a look.'"

It seemed apparent she had seen the view already and wanted me to see it too.

"As I looked out, its beauty left me awestruck. It was beyond anything I had ever seen before (including Lake Louise in the Rockies or the Swiss Alps). It was breath-taking and brought on the most powerful feeling of love inside."

Elinor said she'd had the exact same dream; calculating time differences and dates, we realized it happened at the same time, give or take a few hours. After this, Elinor and I knew without a shadow of a doubt we had a soul assignment together. It was the first time I had ever had an exact same dream with anyone else and it had to have significance.

Elinor joined our community and is offering this work in our 90 Day OPA Global Program. It is unique and definitely brilliantly effective.

The process Elinor works with is not a quick-fix tool—though it can be. It's intricate and sophisticated, accurate and permanent, yet so subtle you hardly recognize its effects at first. Glimpses happen along the way, but where you truly see it is upon reflection in a results review, one, two, or three years later. You discover you have become a completely different person.

When you look back and compare a situation from before and see how you handled it then compared to now, you will find massive changes so big that make a chasm of difference, yet you got nudged along with such baby steps you barely noticed it. The integration happens instantaneously once the shift has occurred. From a marketing point of view, it is a victim of its own brilliance. By this I mean you often do not attribute your changes to this tool because of the quick integration.

The tool builds a person's capacity to handle life better with all its twists and turns, and successes and challenges. It develops your adaptability to change which is a huge asset to have in these changing times. I have become deeply transformed from working with this tool over many years. I love using it because

I never have to stay stuck and can work with it myself, thanks to Elinor's passion in teaching it.

**How does it work?**

Basically, there is a ladder of instincts we move up and down according to what is needed. It happens naturally without any conscious thought. The ladder ranges from Hopeful to Enthusiastic, offering more and more freedom as you climb higher up the ladder. What happens is sometimes we get jammed on at a particular step and we perceive our reality from that vantage point. This is usually very limiting and only half the story. The task to increase your ability is to figure out where you are stuck on the ladder and then shift it with the support of the tool.

To give you an example of how this works, when this process first found me, I was already 10 years into my retreat centre project and was spinning around in a lot of chaos and overwhelmed most of the time. I was jammed on in a particular Instinctive Pattern and it was all about the WE together space. This meant I always needed confirmation and participation from everyone around me before I could move forward with an idea. This more often than not included some of our unsuspecting guests staying at the retreat for a weekend.

What do you think I/we should do?

Until this work with Instinx, I was always looking outside for the answers. With this tool I brought the authority back to myself and my inner guidance. As I worked with the process, I couldn't believe how clearly I could see my next steps and how easy it was to progress in my business and life in general. I noticed how it opens up a kind of inner space where you can hear and see more clearly. I was able to adapt to change quicker and trust myself while in the void. I highly recommend this tool as another way of reaching deeply into where you may be stuck or blind to any given problem. You can find out more about Elinor and her work on our Xenia website.

## *Nature and Silence as Pathways*

Not everyone feels comfortable in nature or with silence when they first turn towards this pathway. The love of nature and silence, though ubiquitous throughout my life, has not always been easy for me either.

I remember one day a lady met me in the parking lot of the retreat centre as she was loading her car to go home. Knowing it was Friday evening and the program hadn't even started yet, I inquired as to why she was leaving. She became a little teary and explained how out of touch with nature she was and didn't feel she had the right to stay. She was feeling the pain of being disconnected from nature and guilty that she had let that happen. Through her tears she said it felt too intimate for her to be here. I told her I related to her story because that had happened to me many years ago. I too had lost touch with this core part of myself and was so sad that I had let it go for so long.

I asked her to stay for even a couple more hours to see if it would be okay.

She did and of course, she stayed the whole weekend and had a wonderful reconnection with her soul.

Now I pay particular attention to my clients and guests when they arrive at Xenia and remember it may be a very intimate thing for them in the beginning. It's as if the veil is so thin in nature that you really feel witnessed and if you are not ready for this it can feel unnerving. It doesn't take long before they start to trust the process and relax into this beautiful available space. In this space you can really find yourself at a much deeper level.

In order to really discover who you are now and what you have to offer the world, it helps to become quiet and listen to the truth from within.

In the silence we can find deeper aspects of ourselves that go beyond the personality traits into our soul. This is where we start to discover who we really are, our true nature.

You don't have to come to my retreat centre to find nature and silence; you can find it everywhere, at a local park in your area or even with animals and plants in your home. It is the essence of this space that holds the magic. We could meditate and walk through a beautiful garden and fall into this space. It doesn't have to be outside us; in fact it isn't ever outside us.

Listening to silence led me to my life's work and I love ushering and holding the space for people to access this fertile ground.

When I was given the vision of Xenia, I was also given three instructions:

1. **Build a Labyrinth,**
2. **Build a Chapel and**
3. **Introduce the work of Silence with everyone you work with.**

When this first got downloaded I was unsure of my ability to hold such a responsibility. It wasn't as if I was great at being silent and I wasn't an avid meditator, but I did love nature and I knew its magic to heal and co-create. It took several years before we started hosting our silent retreats. Now they are a favourite program. Even when working with corporate clients, I do bring at least several hours of silence into the program and it is usually the highlight of the whole experience for them. Sometimes I marvel at how the simplest of things can have the most profound impact. I have now become a big advocate of this amazing tool. Silence is the closest experience to who we really are. This silent space is essential for the integration of the work we do.

## JOURNAL WORK

I suggest downloading the work of Byron Katie and inquire into any beliefs that may be standing in your way.

Take time in nature with a question on your heart and be very attentive to hearing and sensing the answers being given. If you have a Labyrinth[5] in your area, it is an excellent tool for getting clear and relaxing into the creative process. We have one at Xenia open to the public and you can find one in your neighborhood by contacting the link below.

---

[5] https://labyrinthlocator.com

# CHAPTER EIGHT

# Are You Using the Mind or Is It Using You?

As we take space in nature and get more familiar with the silence, we can clearly hear what is going on inside our heads, with all the mind chatter. This chapter is about emerging from the swamp of confusion the mind serves up, into something far deeper that knows the truth and guides us.

Have you noticed when you bring your awareness inwards you can hear a constant dialogue going on in your head from the moment you wake up to the moment you fall asleep? Of course, there is the higher-self mind but that has a different sound and timbre. The ego mind is chit chatting on about this and that. It sounds like a sports commentator reporting every move going on in the room or outside. Most of it is meaningless chatter with no real purpose except to distract you from your essence.

You can be totally thwarted by colluding with what the mind dishes up. I watch the pain and suffering caused when people identify with their mind and believe it is who they are. This is the biggest lie of all when you believe this nonsense. It is not at all who you are.

The mind usually sounds like this:

*You should do this; you shouldn't do that.*

*Who do you think you are?*

*Don't do that, you'll look like a fool.*

*Wow she's fat.*

*He's weird.*

*Wow...I wouldn't do that.*

It is a chiding voice, judgmental, criticizing, and opinionated. Sometimes it pops into our awareness and other times it just rambles on by itself. It may be in the tone of a parent or teacher or some person we have idolized on TV. We may be comforted by a familiar voice that feels like ourselves, our main personality. Even so, it is not who we truly are.

**Watch out for the voice of the Saboteur.**

One day a man arrived at my retreat centre, having heard me give a talk earlier that summer. He was curious to visit Xenia and tracked me down to connect with me again.

After showing him around a little, we sat in the dining room talking and I could see and feel he was in a great deal of distress. His head was slumped down and he was constantly berating himself for some past deed. He sounded and acted like a very young boy with very little confidence. I gleaned he was some kind of retired engineer as he mentioned an invention he had regarding sustainable energy.

This was followed by a rash of reasons about why he couldn't possibly share it, like he wasn't good enough to present it to the world. His programming and internal dialogue clogged any possibility of him honouring his Calling and standing behind this invention. He seemed locked in a self-destructive pattern and my knee jerk reaction was to counsel him. Of course, he had not asked for this and I realized there was nothing really wrong here – even if he did appear in pain.

Suddenly the thought came that I should be present with him and invite him to be present also. At first this was not easy since he seemed deeply committed to his self- implosion. How do I stay out of his business and simply be here now? I wondered. Slowly I became aware of the leaves dancing across the meadow in the wind and the horses grazing outside. I invited him to look out the window, which he did willingly. As he looked up, his energy started to shift.

Next the attention moved to what was in the room and on the table and before long he actually looked at me for the first time since arriving two hours earlier. His eyes locked onto mine and I could feel him let go and relax. I simply held the stillness and felt compassion arising.

Tears started running down his cheeks and a smile opened his face. No content was required. I knew he had arrived in the present moment and a new reference point was born.

I saw the power of this transformation and it was without the usual techniques, content, analysis, and work. It was simple, non-intrusive, and graceful. A shift had occurred for this man and a shift had occurred in my life as well. I noticed how presence is intelligence and that all I had to do was get out of the way and be the witness, the sanctuary, for the other. In this way, the space becomes available for whatever wants to move into it. I've always wondered what happened to him and what difference it made to be witnessed that day.

## *Meditation Pathway*

Meditation is a great way to become aware of the mind and there are so many different ways to practice meditation. I will not be teaching a particular way here other than the simplest way I do it. My practice is more of a mindfulness practice. I have a ritual in the mornings when I awaken. I make my tea, light a candle, and sit quietly to begin my day. Often, I will have my dog on one side and my cat on the other, and together we sit quietly for 20 minutes or so.

Next, living at the retreat centre we do have wonderful Sanctuaries where I love to meditate quietly and become attuned to the beautiful silence. I also walk my dog around the lake every day and this too is a form of meditation. When I groom my horse, I consciously make a point of becoming really present with him, especially when I am riding him. Awareness is highly important and what I love about it is it brings me closer and connected to myself as I connect with him.

For some reason I have never been drawn to any kind of dogma or strict regimes, but I do appreciate those people who have the discipline to practice whatever it is that resonates for them.

There are some beings who have reached the point of enlightenment and say they no longer have this kind of thinking going on from the ego. Others report they are aware of the mind rambling on but have learned to not give it their attention and especially not believe anything it is saying.

We can meditate anywhere, anytime, and you can train the mind when you are aware of its commentary and concerns. In many ways, it is attempting to serve us and protect us, though it is annoying most of the time. The mind can really scare us if we are unconscious of the fact that its job is to hide our essence as a way of protecting us when we are absent. We have been told the mind is the enemy and it needs to be annihilated but the truth is, it is a useful tool and deserves our respect.

*So, the question is: Are you using the mind or is the mind using you?*

Is it Friend or Foe? Give the mind a job to do. This could be witnessing your breathing or helping visualize a manifestation you would like from your deep core of awareness, which is the only place worth manifesting from.

When I was going through my dark night of the soul, precipitated by the fraudulent mortgage investment, I was literally brought to my knees with terror. The terror was caused by believing what the mind was telling me would happen if I didn't get the money that was needed.

The fear about money was devastating and I will share more about this experience in Chapter 8. I don't know if you have noticed how the story the mind tells you gets amplified at night. I would lie awake at night and scare the life out of myself regarding my money situation. One night I decided the stress was too much to bear and decided to take charge of my mind. I made a rule that I would not allow any thoughts about money at night. So every time I heard:

You're going to lose your retreat centre, you're in trouble...etc....etc....etc., I simply dismissed it right away.

No. No. No, I would say. In the beginning it was a matter of becoming aware and as soon as that happened I had the power to stop it. Many times I fell into the mind's spell and let it torture me. Then I started to realize something in my psyche was really scared and like a child I started negotiating with this small part within.

I made an agreement that it was not allowed to go on about money at night if I also agreed to address the problem by day. In other words, if there was a true and legitimate problem I was avoiding, I would have to answer the questions and fears the mind was presenting by day, as agreed. This started to be like a partnership with the mind. And I had to be impeccable about this agreement. I noticed how quickly I mastered this response from the mind and to this day (15 years later), I do not hear any commentary about money at night.

If I do, then I take it up immediately with my accounting people to ease my mind about our finances. Does that make sense to you? Now if you are not familiar with inner child work and accessing parts of yourself, I highly recommend you befriend this notion and embrace it. I always include it in the programs I offer because it is a fundamental part of our emotional well-being.

I deduced from this exercise that if I could take control over my thinking at night, I can do it during the day as well.

This whole exercise is about bringing awareness to that which isn't working in our lives and how to solve it. By listening to the mind and clearing beliefs, patterns, and inner child fears, we can be current in our lives and empowered to live the life we were born to live, at any age.

JOURNAL WORK

If you find yourself wide awake at night worrying about money or anything, the first step is to become aware. If you keep paper and pen beside your bed, you can make notes about specific worries of the mind. It's like telling the worried child that you have made a note of it and everything will be okay. Next, practice mindfulness by feeling your body in the bed and really giving it your full attention for a while. Remember the next day to take this information seriously and decide if something further needs to be done.

# CHAPTER NINE

# The Illusion of Time and Money

*"What we really want to do is what we are really meant to do. When we do what we are meant to do, money comes to us, doors open for us, we feel useful, and the work we do feels like play to us."* — Julia Cameron

## *Regarding Money*

Do you believe you are not living your dream and doing your soul work now because of money? Are you afraid your retirement plan isn't adequate, so you have to keep doing what you know? Maybe you are already retired but afraid to invest funds towards something as frivolous as your passion and longing. Maybe you have conditioning and rules that say bad things could happen if you don't have enough money. Or maybe you have all the money in the world to be able to do whatever you choose when you chose but still something called "It's about money," raises its head.

Well the truth of the matter is, *It's never about the money*. Now this may sound like a contradiction to the earlier Maslow Hierarchy of Needs, but I am asking you to look a little deeper here. Check around and see if your needs are in fact being met financially. Most people reading this book probably have a roof over their head and food on their table. Is taking your next step towards your Calling going to break you financially? Don't ask your mind. Ask your heart.

It's a great exercise to explore your beliefs and conditioning about money in general and specifically your earliest memory. This memory is ripe with clues about how you have and are living your life in the area of money.

I've heard financial advisers say our earliest memories of money often play a significant role in how we view money later on in life. It's amazing how much the mind can play a role in creating or destroying financial freedom. These money memories have such a hold on our lives—they directly impact our relationship with money.

### Earliest Memory about Money:

For me, the understanding of money and abundance took hold at an early age. I was five years old when something magical happened for me. It was my earliest memory about money and as always, a belief pattern got set in that would deepen throughout my life.

My parents had taken my sister and me with them to Dad's local club for a lunchtime drink. Kids were not really allowed in there, but people turned a blind eye. From this very young age I enjoyed watching adults and this day I was curious about the machines they were using. They put money in and pulled a handle and these different fruit images rolled around and around until they stopped. I asked my mum what they were doing, and she said, 'They're giving their money to the children in need.'

Maybe she didn't think I'd understand, but what she said seemed believable to me. Wow, this is great, I thought, "I want to give my money to them as well." On top of the machine stood a little cardboard box with a picture of a child with their leg in a brace (polio), and I figured it must be to help her get better. My memory of what happened next is still vivid.

I pulled a chair across the room, so I could reach the machine. My mum gave me a sixpenny bit from my pocket money and I put it in the slot, pulled the handle, (with Dad's help as I recall) and we watched the apples, pears, and oranges going around until they stopped. Just as I started climbing down from the chair, a parade of lights and bells went off, as all these little silver sixpenny bits came tumbling out of the machine. It startled me and everyone else. Dad said I had hit the jackpot!

At the time, I had no idea what had happened but later came to realize the impact it had on my life. I thought I was helping somebody and won a jackpot instead. Jackpots became a theme throughout my life and I took it to be normal.

Where I really started to understand the story of money was a time in my life that brought me to my knees in a dark night of the soul. Do you remember when I talked about having a dark night of the soul experience that I resolved but there lingered a story for a few years about it? Here is what happened.

After spending eleven years and hundreds of thousands of dollars transforming an old broken down dilapidated 38-acre sheep farm into a beautiful retreat centre, I suffered severe financial loss that put my vision in jeopardy. This was due to a fraudulent $350,000 mortgage investment trust that was exposed and precipitated a downward domino effect. There was a hemorrhage going on and I needed to grow up and learn how to run my business. I was blocked from receiving or learning by this crippling fear.

I was five months behind in the mortgage, three years behind in property taxes; receiving disconnection notices and for the life of me, I couldn't find the money to make ends meet and stop the downward spiral. This whole process took about two years and I was living in fear every day, which amped up to three months of sheer terror when I learned my beloved Xenia was going into the newspaper for a tax sale.

Somehow, I knew this terror was bigger than just losing a property; it was like losing a child. How could it be I would lose Xenia after a decade of hard work and great programs happening? It felt as if it were meant to exist to do powerful work like the programs we were doing empowering street kids and helping adults to heal through a plethora of challenges. In short, it was providing transformation for thousands of people who came and found healing and solace. It didn't make sense. How could it be over?

I continued to run from the terror, begging people to help me, trying to sell things and get bank loans, but to no avail. My best friend was cleaning houses and giving me money for food and my daughter was baby-sitting to help out while at one point I literally sat comatose on the couch. I was stuck in this abiding darkness until the stress became too heavy to bear and finally, I gave myself to the terror in absolute surrender.

It was like fire consuming me totally and completely until there was nothing left. No more fear, no more bag lady stories, no more Xenia, no more body. It didn't matter anymore. The fight was over. The white flag had been raised. What remained was a quiet space. Stillness. It felt like a death.

From then on, I simply followed instructions from this deep pool of listening.

The next day with total ease and grace, my soul sister Ariel and I raised $20,000 of gifted money in three and a half hours. We put the mortgage back on track and never looked back.

What a drastic difference from begging and pleading to complete acceptance in a moment. After the surrender I was clearly and purely in service. It was no longer my plan but Thy plan. I learned you cannot solve money problems with money. That was like pouring money into the void and why people wouldn't give me money with the repelling energy I had been holding in the fear state. After this complete surrender, the space opened for me to receive and all the help I needed arrived. This whole experience changed my life forever. I understood the money game in a whole new way and it was all about energy and what I was standing in.

I don't wish for you to go through this experience but if that's what it takes to surrender and wake up, I say: bring it on. Today I am grateful for this massive lesson because I learned I alone cannot do anything, and it was about trusting in a higher power to guide and support me. I lean into this 100% today in everything I do.

I have noticed we are never led astray when the urge comes from within to act. It may seem uncomfortable or crazy but by now you probably have concluded the theme in this book is about courage and radical trust. If what you want to do next feels a little out there or even like an insane idea, see if you have a money story that may be blocking your progress.

Here are some questions to consider in identifying your money story:

- What would you consider a normal way of viewing money in your life?
- What was your earliest memory about money?
- What did you hear and see as a child in your household about money?

- When did you first hold physical money in your hands?
- Were you given an allowance, and did you have to work for it?
- Was it regarded as your money? In other words, were you able to spend it or save it?
- What beliefs did you pick up from your parents? I.e.: money is bad, money is evil, money doesn't grow on trees or come from thin air.
- Did you ever consider your family rich or poor before the age of 12?
- Did your parents reference rich people as bad, good etc.?
- Did money influence your choice of careers? I.e. going to university?
- What are the feelings you carry in your body and soul from these earliest memories? Are they shameful, guilt based, or enjoyable and freeing?

- What is your relationship with money? How do you feel about it and how easily can you manifest it?

- Are your financial needs being met?

I received a very large inheritance which allowed me to manifest this wonderful dream-come-true of my retreat centre. For many years it didn't feel like mine because my husband had had to die for it to be realized. In other words, I didn't deserve it because I hadn't "earned it," in the traditional sense.

And that is partly also why I lost $350,000 – I couldn't accept the full amount of money that came to me. Many people who receive inheritances or win large jackpots have found ways to get rid of the money as quickly as possible because they didn't have the experience or mindset to carry that much wealth.

I had a lot of work to do to accept and receive this gift. When it really changed for me was when I earned my first one million dollars in my relationship marketing business. It was after achieving this success that I knew I could earn serious wealth with my skills and abilities rather than it being given to me. It was a significant turning point and allowed me to steward my retreat centre in a more empowered way.

And what I love is the more I receive, the more I can share with others and create in ways that will serve. If your dream requires a lot of money, consider being a receiving tower of abundance for this to actualize. I know the more we share our gifts and impact the lives of others, the more abundance flows to us.

I started this section by saying it is never about the money. I want to explain this a little further here. When we honour our Calling and feel the impulse to act rather than resist, the money will show up for it. If it is part of the divine plan, it has to.

There was a course I wanted to attend that cost $15,000 US ($20,000 Canadian). At the time there was no way I could "afford' it," especially since we needed new roofing on a couple of the buildings and the septic system needed help. I had a daughter getting married and many other expenses on the table. If I were to listen to financial advisers, it would have been wrong to proceed. But I knew with every cell of my being I was supposed to do the program and it was part of my future work, so I said yes before I had any idea where the money would come from.

As it turned out, my retreat centre business rocketed during the next few months, so much so that the profit more than covered the cost of this course. It was so graphic I tracked the manifestation:

1. Seeing clearly what I wanted.
2. Feeling the truth from my heart that it was aligned.
3. Staying 100% impeccable with the plan. Not once letting any negative dialogue creep in. Saying *Yes & Now*. Or wherever needed, your healthy *No*.
4. Proceeding first and letting the money catch up.

Now I know your conditioning may have a problem with this idea and want to tell you all the reasons this is stupid. But I have witnessed it time and time again when something feels so important and I just proceed towards the plan as if the money were already there. And guess what? It is. And of course, my basic financial needs were totally being met, even if my mind had another opinion.

I can cite hundreds of times I have experienced this and also witnessed it in others. The most important part is impeccable and consistent handling of the mind once you have clarity of purpose and permission to proceed from within.

## Regarding Time

*Time is a created thing. To say, 'I don't have time,' is like saying, 'I don't want to. —Lao Tzu*

You say you do not have enough time, or this is not the time. Yet time ticks on and soon you are wondering if your dream is ever going to happen. Will you ever go for what you want? When people tell me they don't have time, I know they are simply saying I don't want to. I wish they would tell the truth instead of using lame excuses about time.

What if time didn't actually exist and you are making it all up? Let me explain what I mean by this. What if absolutely everything that has ever happened was exactly as it was supposed to happen, when it happened? There was never a mistake. We are not a mistake and there could never be a mistake. If you go from that premise (and humour me if you cannot even imagine this concept), then that means you have a blank canvas right now in front of you, yours to create with.

Imagine if suddenly the red light turns green and you can proceed. What if this is your call and permission to proceed? Not that you need it from me, but it may help.

When you shatter the illusion of *there is never a right time to do what you love*, and place it as a priority, the process is set in motion. But if you need to control all of your outside circumstances first, you may never wake up and live the life you were born to live.

One of my dear friends retired from nursing after 30+ years. There was a big celebration party and excitement about her starting another business and her new life as a facilitator and author. I was so happy for her to finally be freed up from this very demanding role she had been playing for decades. Several months later when I tried to set up a luncheon with her, she was too busy working. I inquired as to what she was working on and found out she started taking more and more shifts back at the hospital and before long she was doing nursing full time again. WHY?

Was it the money? No, remember it is never about the money. It may have been the security and comfort level she felt in this career of familiarity. Even though she reported it wasn't enjoyable any more, I guess she wasn't quite ready to make the change.

Confidence and willingness to jump into your heart's work is a very fragile place for you to be that vulnerable. Often this is because you have been damaged regarding your gifts and talents. I'm sorry if this happened to you. It did happen to me.

Writing has been a passion of mine since I was a young girl. I always knew I was born to write books, but it wasn't until reaching nearly 60 that I wrote my first book.

The damage that happened to me impacted my life from the moment the energy break occurred at age eight. I wrote something at school for my dad and took it home full of delight to share it with him. He read it as I sat looking up at him with eager anticipation and what happened next traumatized me. He scolded me and sent me out to the back garden saying I didn't write it and I must have gotten an older girl to write it for me. I was devastated, thinking perhaps I didn't write it after all. It swooped through me with such ease it felt like it was someone else writing it. I spent most of my life doubting what I had to say and write and had to do a lot of healing work to be able to put pen to paper. Or more accurately, I did write, I wrote a lot but never ever shared any of my writings, up until three years ago. Better late than never, I would say.

Nothing can fill the emptiness but the dream or passion we tossed aside as unfit or unimportant. When I write now—and this is my third book—I am in bliss and know all is well in the world. I am finally doing what I came to planet earth to do without apologizing for it. I bet you even have a book in you. Your forte is so deeply connected within you that you may actually think it's not that big a deal. We sometimes think everyone can do what we do, when in fact they cannot. They especially cannot do it the way you do it. Your gift is so natural and enjoyable that you often put it in the category of being selfish or 'I should be doing something more important.'

What if your contribution is a vital part of humanity? You may think that is a little grandiose, but I truly believe it is so.

When is the time to begin? I would say *Yes & Now*.

JOURNAL WORK

Take some time to journal your answers from the questions in this chapter. This will reveal so much information for you to work with and inquire into. Once you see the beliefs you hold about money, time, and energy, you may be shocked by what was running underground in your life. It may explain why your money story is the way it is.

# CHAPTER TEN

# Who or What Do You Need to Forgive?

*The Unwillingness to forgive another, is a curse upon yourself. –Marshall Vian Summers*

Why does forgiveness have anything to do with honouring your Calling? Good question. Forgiveness liberates your soul and removes barriers to living your dream. When you live in a state of not forgiving, you leak power. When you live in what should have been or could have been, you leak power too. This may be standing in the way of you not having taken the steps towards your Calling. I wanted to bring awareness to forgiveness because it can make or break your ability to deliver your jewel to the world. If you have a person or situation needing forgiveness, it is important to discover it and learn how to free yourself from any burden you are carrying in this way.

In order to forgive, first stop identifying yourself with the suffering that was caused to you. Whenever you allow a hurt or deep wound to live in you without understanding, it takes up space and eats away at your life force.

Not forgiving someone does not hurt them at all but it does hurt you when you harbor resentment and never let it go. You are the one carrying the heavy burden—how crazy is that? It is part of the jail bars created and why you are not free to move on. I have seen people get sick and hold back their dreams for a lifetime because of their undercover (or so they think) rage about a father or mother or some other situation that they have not yet met with understanding. And true understanding needs movement to occur for it to be complete. Understanding without action is not true understanding at all.

If you have been around the block of personal development you probably discovered techniques and systems to help you forgive. You may have already done your forgiveness work, and all should be well. And maybe it is. The best way to know if you have released the apparent crime the other has imposed on you is to look at the results. How do you feel when you think of that person? Really and deeply feel this and you will know the truth. If when you think of them you are neutral or even loving, then the work is done. Sometimes we think by eclipsing that person right out of our lives it takes care of the problem, but unfortunately it does not. It doesn't just involve the physical presence; it is the emotional energetics and spiritual side that needs to be addressed.

I first heard Byron Katie talk about forgiveness as: *"Forgiveness is seeing that what you thought happened didn't."* At first I was a little perturbed, I must admit, but soon I started to understand the real meaning behind her words. It's not to say the awful abuse that was done to a person didn't actually happen; it is more that it didn't happen exactly and completely and for the reasons that person may have thought.

There is so much more to the entire story. Especially the fact that it is in the past and no matter how you may beg, wish, pray, or manipulate it, you cannot change what happened. It is already done. However changing the way you look at it can begin the thaw as you examine the deeper truth. You can actually liberate yourself completely from the perceived transgression and even find gifts that happened as a result. Crazy I know, but as you inquire into it, you will be surprised what you will find.

I simply love Wayne Dyer's famous quote: When you change the way you look at things, the things you look at change.

There was a time where I was invited to a big event and learned that a person who had done a complete character assassination on me years earlier was going to be in attendance. At first, I was pissed off they were invited and even approached the host asking her to uninvite them. After all she did know the circumstances of my request. I felt insecure and defensive. So, I imagined being there and determined not to talk to her just simply avoid her. That would take care of it, wouldn't it, I thought.

Knowing I had obviously hit a core wound I sat with the feelings associated with it instead.

The next morning, I did an Instinx process and found where I was stuck. Right away I shifted with the tool and the difference I felt from this was profound. I was able to adapt to the situation. The first thing I noticed was I actually felt love and compassion for this person. I knew she was really fear based and had slandered me out of a place of ignorance. I considered this and knew she did not even know me at all. There was a peace and spaciousness I felt inside and knew that no matter what, I would not need to avoid this person. They would be welcome in my space.

I realized the notion Maya Angelou spoke of: when people gossip or slander you, you are not in it. In other words, it says more about them than you. You are only in it if you put yourself there. I saw this to be totally true to the point that I literally looked forward to seeing this person at the event.

When I saw her I wasn't exactly lovey, dovey but I was respectful and kind. I was free. As it turned out it was a wonderful and very loving event that healed the situation completely.

Our feelings will lead us to our unconscious beliefs, which are the barriers or guards standing in the way of our freedom and happiness. And remember, as we track our feelings we have to also consider that they are not an accurate gauge upon which to act. But to feel our feelings with awareness rather than explaining them away, is the key.

## *Forgiving Ourselves*

Ultimately, it is usually our self we haven't forgiven for whatever indiscretion may have happened in our lives. I had one client who woke up 32 years later from his career and realized he had followed in his father's footsteps as a dentist. when all along he was a renaissance man and brilliant videographer and musician. He longed his whole life to do his own thing but his programming and responsibility as a father took precedence. Once he became aware of living someone else's dream, he was in a grieving process for quite some time. For a while he was deeply upset and blamed and criticized himself for not doing what he wanted. I assured him through our work together that he had accomplished an incredible career and served hundreds, maybe thousands of people with his very caring heart and skill. He had provided a great lifestyle for his family and it was the exact perfect thing to do then. Now is now, but not to make what happened wrong. That again is insanity. I guess he wasn't to become aware of living his passion until it was the right time later in life.

The good news is he is now aware and already started on his inspired book and course regarding photography and capturing the essence in people and places through the lens. He is stoked and his whole demeanor has changed. I am happy for him for his new life and at the same time he can feel proud of all that he has done to bring him to this place on his life's journey.

JOURNAL WORK

Where do you still need to forgive yourself or another? Dig in deeply here because it could be the most important key to unlock your treasure. Make a list of all the significant people throughout your life and tick them off one at a time, but not before you thoroughly investigate the energy stored in your being about them. Remember if it is not either neutral or loving, the energy about them has not been cleared.

Word of caution: the mind can be slippery and deceitful. Don't override a feeling with your mind. And, don't let your mind interpret your feelings. Simply feel them with as much awareness as you can muster.

# CHAPTER ELEVEN

# Trusting Love

Why is trusting love important to our Calling and living our dream mission?

Well I would say it has everything to do with how we show up and the degree by which we are free to really go for it in life. As a single person it is great in many ways because we are freer to make decisions for ourselves, whereas with a partner, we have them to consider as well. As a couple it can be exponentially powerful, as in when two or more are gathered, or it can be difficult, like pushing a boulder up a hill if you are held back by the insecurities of your significant other.

In one of my programs there was a couple who had been together for years and there was so much friction between them. He was a retired police officer who had spent years recovering from burn out from the extreme events he lived through on the job. He was now at a stage of blossoming and wanting to begin his new life.

Being a person of great service, this was his wish and he was looking for new ways to do that. His wife was also in the program (under duress) and it was painful to witness the deep insecurity she displayed by her facial gestures and intense discomfort every time he spoke in the circle. She sat in resentment for most of the program. I could see by his weight gain and declining health he was stuck between wanting to please her and wanting to break free.

This is a dilemma I have witnessed many times and it sometimes happens that a breakthrough occurs for both parties and sometimes it does not. Partnership work is such an important aspect of our programs because it sits at the core of our ability to respond to do what we came here to do.

Opening my heart to intimate love was a struggle for most of my life. It was partly because I have always been so mission driven and I didn't want anything or anyone getting in the way of that. But the greater reason was that I did not trust love. Not until way later did it ever occur to me that a healthy aligned partner could actually support and enhance my mission. Alignment is the key.

When I look back on my life and think about all the different relationships and experiences I have been through, I could judge myself harshly, but when I view it through the lens of everything happening for a reason, I have to view it differently.

My relationship experiences were rocky at best. It seemed like intimate relationships were my nemesis in this lifetime. There were some lovely men who adored me and clearly wanted to support me that I couldn't let in. There were others who wanted to own me and were unable to truly love me and I picked them. My experiences usually were with men who didn't actually get me at all and certainly were not capable of supporting me without a big agenda. I learned this in my childhood through my parental role modeling. I was caught in the cycle of creating the classic fairy tale dream only to plummet into desperate betrayal and abandonment.

Finally, I learned about trusting love as truth through a very difficult relationship. This relationship progressed rapidly, including into marriage, when the door got suddenly slammed shut on the second day of the honeymoon when he disappeared emotionally and then physically several months later. I was totally devastated, and it took at least three years to get over the pain in my heart.

For a very long time, I believed it was my fault and I had done something wrong. I painfully went through scenarios from the past, investigating what I could have done better. I had been so certain that he loved me. I started to doubt my heart and my loving and even became cynical of love. In fact, so much so, I stayed away from intimate relationships for over a decade after that experience.

Then one day this same man returned into my life and we had many conversations via phone and Skype, since he lived on another continent. I noticed my heart and soul were so happy and excited. I figured if he showed up in my life again, there must be a reason. I suspected it could even have been to clean up the gap of misunderstanding so I could heal my cynicism. And being a born optimist, I even wondered if now we could be together. We did have a common mission regarding a transformational tool and I let myself be seduced by my own thinking. It could work out even though there were serious red flags.

One day in a long email, he admitted he was still in love with me and was open to coming back to Canada to be with me. There was a sweet humbleness in his words that moved me deeply. He sounded like he had insight about what had happened previously. Of course, I was a bit weary and didn't want to be an idiot, but I became hopeful.

It was in about the third month of many three-hour long conversations by Skype, when he sent me a dozen beautiful red roses and a card expressing his love for me. As crazy as it may sound, I felt I could trust the situation. My heart and soul knew his heart and soul and it was pure. In spite of friends and family telling me to be careful, they also supported me because they trusted what life was bringing to me and they felt I had enough self-awareness to handle whatever came up.

After the roses, I didn't hear from him again for over a month and I was really sad but kept honoring his need for space and time. Then there were a few more correspondences and then nothing again. One day I was driving through town and I knew something was off. Something weird was going on and I could feel it in the pit of my stomach. Insistent on clarity, I asked the Angels to please help, to give me a message, a sign. I was emphatic it had to be crystal clear and immediate. Bossy, I know, but I needed to know the truth.

I was not prepared for what happened next. When I arrived home and checked my emails, I received one from him revealing that this relationship was over and could never go forward again.

I was in a state of shock for about three days while I tried to unravel all of the assumptions and expectations I had.

There was a big difference this time—I didn't throw myself away. I didn't separate from myself by blaming him or myself. I knew I had shown up fully. I knew I was ready to go the distance and do the work.

As much as I knew this truth, I noticed my mind wanted to accuse me of being wrong again about the love I felt from him and for him and I wanted to totally invalidate it. How could I have been so wrong again? What an idiot, the mind harangued. When would I wake up out of attracting these types of unavailable partners? Then deeply I felt the words: *When I loved and trusted myself enough. When I knew I deserved better, that's when!*

Sitting in the pain for a few days, I reached out for guidance from a clear guide, Jean Christian.[6]
*Here are a few excerpts from the reading.*
*To never, never doubt the love your heart held and holds. Love is to be understood here. Not to be viewed as being deluded or a great mistake on your part. To not do that to your heart, to your being that knew love. The love was a real flow for you and link for you and for him.*
*And here it must be appreciated that every being, every soul is in a process through unconsciousness to consciousness. And through pain into liberation, suffering into freedom. Do not discount that he was resonant and is resonant to you, from soul to soul. That this love was true and real. For him not to doubt his love, is his journey. For you not to doubt your love*

---

[6] Jean S. Christian http://www.becomingtruth.com

is your journey. Do not doubt the information the heart knows, or the soul knows.

Time must be taken to learn, in an intimate relationship, how well is this being, how thorough is their ability to be fully aware of who they are, both in their process, in their beauty and in their pain and suffering. For any relationship will live and grow and thrive if the person is ready to see and accept and to know what their unconsciousness looks like and feels like.

So they can speak about it and can have it pointed to and can point to it themselves. And can be going into spiritual practice towards dispelling that. A relationship that becomes an impossibility is when it does eclipse into a non-recognition or denial.  Into such a duality when one moment they know themselves and then in the next moment they know not.

So, the lesson is to choose the one to walk with that closely, is well enough.  Has had enough consciousness practice either in this lifetime and before so that they can be aware of their own shadows, aware of their own being and not put it onto another. And not create dramatic events that make no sense.

For you to go from this experience forward with a real honoring of your ability to love the reality of, and validation of your love. To not even use any words, like: I was deluded, I was crazy, I made a big mistake. Rather to go forward to say next time I feel so much love, I will be patient and I will take time to know more deeply how well and ready is this person to

*stay in this love. To work with their shadows, their*
*unconsciousness openly and together. And to know the*
*fullness of who the person is before going ahead.*
*Trust your love and tell everyone through your books and*
*work. When you love, trust it. You can love the most broken*
*person who you could never marry but you can love them*
*because you see their soul and they can see yours. Love itself is*
*unqualified, unnamed. It isn't about friendship or marriage*
*nor therapy, love is just a force of resonance. Where the*
*discernment comes in is what to do with this love. Two levels*
*of it. One is the pure unnameable. One is the discerning of*
*what sort of relationship to go into. But never editing the*
*message of the heart when it feels the surge, the stream, the*
*resonance of love to another being. This is to be trusted all the*
*time. The only place to put the question of trust is where do I*
*go with this, what is this relationship supposed to be? If this*
*is a client then this is as far as this is to go. If it is a friend, I*
*am here forever to walk with you and come into your home*
*and assist you when things are dark. If this is a marriage then*
*this needs to be with a person that is as well as I am, as ready*
*as I am, to be continuous and steady in how we create life*
*together.*

Silence prevailed as I absorbed the words from
this guidance and recognized the truth. I knew I had
misunderstood what was possible with this man and

our love. Not the love itself. This was truly profound to hear and see from a different perspective. Now I have been awoken to the discernment factor.

I thought going through this whole heartbreak one more time would have furthered amped up my cynicism, but it did the opposite. It liberated me through the understanding. Not right or wrong, good or bad, just seeing clearly what the truth was. I knew this time I had not abandoned myself like before. I trusted it was all part of the awakening journey. No guilt, no blame, no shame. Just what was arising.

The true forgiveness came about for me a year later and it brought about a complete transfiguration. I was at a program in Arizona doing some work with Nancy Shipley Rubin[7] and we did an exercise where I got to enact the situation with my ex with a surrogate. He didn't know the facts at all and it was totally surprising how intuitively he played his part excellently and accurately.

I started feeling angry and shouted at him: *Why did you have to leave?*

---

[7] http://www.rubinenterprises.info

He said: *I had to.*

I was mad and said I didn't understand.

He shared: *I couldn't go any further, it was too hard for me.*

It took a few minutes as we bantered back and forth but as this was happening something was stirring in my heart as I started to understand the truth and I saw he couldn't go any further. It wasn't "his fault." As the understanding moved through my entire body and soul, I felt my heart open and love flooded in. I felt such compassion for him and forgiveness for us both, knowing he had travelled as far with me as he was able to. It was not a mistake or wrong, it just was the end of the road and as far as our destiny together went.

The good news is it totally unhooked me from my cynicism about love and I knew my heart was fully opened again.

Greater things can come when we open up the space by forgiving. Our personal power returns and we are freed up to pursue our dreams. Love is the great healer and we all have the power to heal any pain inflicted upon us with love. Tracking this configuration was important and I offer it to you for any unforgiving situation standing in your way.

- Feel the Feeling (blame, resentment, anger)
- Identify Belief associated with Feeling (you abandoned me, I'm unlovable etc.)
- Catch a glimpse of understanding, if you can. (If not, stay with the process.)
- Feel the acceptance rising as you get to the truth of the situation. You cannot change the past or change or fix the "other."
- Feel the compassion because your heart opens up and you meet the situation with real understanding. Grace takes care of the rest.

**Does your Calling (dream) include a partner?** Or maybe you already have this supportive person in your life.

I don't think I ever felt stopped by the relationships I had but I did notice I played a much smaller game with some of them. In other words, I held myself back based on what I thought they wanted. The trouble with this is that it hinders our freedom to really go for our Calling if we are not aligned in partnership with one who can embrace us fully.

A great question to ask our self is:

*Do you shrink or expand in this person's presence?*

I am not advocating getting rid of unsupportive relationships – this is not that book, but I am pointing out the importance of this. Ultimately it is never the other that stops us, it is our self. However, life gets better when we are honouring each other instead of restricting and sabotaging our efforts.

Notice if you felt held back. Maybe it is just a matter of being courageous and asking for what you need and going for it.

If you are not presently with a significant other and feel ready to have one, remember what the guidance showed me. Love is real and true, discernment of what that relationship is, is the question to be answered.

## *True Alignment*

Shortly after learning this profoundly important lesson, my wonderful partner Alexander entered my life. I first met him poised behind a camera at the barn, getting a candid shot of me with my horse. Later I saw his passion for photography and was in awe of what he produced when he storied his photos together and married them with music.

He seems nice, I thought, and kind. Those were my first few ponderings.

Over the next two years we would become friends and have a lot of fun together. I learned while talking and walking around the lake how he was healing from his broken marriage and he was fully into his personal development and spiritual journey. I liked him and made a special note about my feelings towards him.

It so happened we have the same birthday, February 8th, and a couple of years earlier while on a trip to India, Alexander FaceTimed me from the Taj Mahal. It was so sweet and again something deep stirred inside me about this man.

We even went dancing at my friend's band event and it was fantastic – he loved to dance and we danced really well together. Again, I couldn't help but wonder what a great match we would be.

I didn't receive any cues from him or energy of attraction but more just friends enjoying each other's company. Both being Aquarians, this would not be hard to imagine. Many of my girlfriends could see what a great match we would be and said I should give him a sign that I was interested. No, I said, it isn't the right time.

Now, I didn't have any clue what I was saying but that's how it felt, and I kept letting the whole thing go, never dwelling on it for more than a moment here and there.

January 1st, 2018 foreshadowed a change. It was the best ever New Year's event. Nine of us had a wonderful medicine pipe ceremony in the Sanctuary followed by a candlelit Labyrinth walk. In the centre we started singing, and we sang and sang in full exuberance for an hour while we heard locals sending up fireworks into the crisp full moonlit air. Again, I made a special note of how easy it was to have Alexander be a part of these celebrations.

That night, I had a dream about Alexander: He was wearing a red scarf around his head and dancing up and down inviting me to lighten up. He was dancing like a clown and smiling from ear to ear. "Let's have fun, Angelyn," he said.

On Jan. 1st before we went in search of the Mastodon[8] on Bowen Island, I shared my dream with Alexander and he happened to be wearing a red scarf. He immediately placed the scarf around his head and there he was, just like the dream. He was a jester ready to play and still not knowing what was coming in just a few short days.

## Moment of Soul Recognition

Five days later, Alexander was driving me back to the ferry after an event we attended in Vancouver. We decided to have fish and chips at Horseshoe Bay before I boarded the ferry. During dinner Alexander shared some stories of his childhood and particularly how he felt as a young boy in school. My heart opened as I felt the vulnerability of this man remembering his childhood. Suddenly we glanced into each other's left eye and that's when it happened. We saw into each other for the first time at the heart and soul level. It was a soul recognition moment.

---

[8] Mastodon on Bowen Island https://www.youtube.com/watch?v=duSFzfv-TEl

Alexander said: "There you are," and we continued to stare for another moment or two without saying anything further about it. Awkwardly we got the bill, paid, packed up, and went for a walk down by the Bay before he escorted me back to the ferry.

I insisted that he could leave me there, even though the ferry wasn't due for another 45 minutes. I could tell he wanted to wait with me, but I gently sent him on his way.

Wow, what just happened? I thought. My heart had been opened and I could feel the warmth and love flowing through my entire being, I didn't realize how shut down and guarded I had been for so many years, or at least that it showed.

Text: three hours later:

Al: Thank you for letting me in today to see the infinite beauty of your heart....

It feels like I ought to have waited with you for the ferry.

An: It's okay.

Al: Hmm.

An: Yes, I guess that was a sweet moment in the restaurant and then it felt a little awkward leaving.

Al: Yup…if you are open to more 'sweet moments' there is lots to explore.

An: I'm open

Al: Yeah

Al: Where shall we go from her? Would you like to chat?

Next, we had a one-hour phone call and before we hung up the phone, he invited me to join him on a trip to Cabo for our joint birthday, which was only one month away.

Yikes, talk about fast and jumping in quickly, but it felt different this time since we had been friends already for a couple of years. I figured the very worst that could happen is we would have fun no matter what. If we didn't connect romantically it would still be okay.

The next morning, we booked our trip to Cabo. Talk about Radical Trust.

It turned out to be the perfect trip. We were in a beautiful bubble as we got to know each other in an intimate way. We have been together ever since, and gratitude is the state we feel the most in this union.

We are aligned with our Calling, which makes it exponentially marvelous and fun. I feel respected and cared for like never before and I feel the strength of supporting each other in a common mission that can impact the world.

The glue that sits at the foundation of our relationship, is the knowing that we have a purpose together. To support each other to honour our Calling. We feel led by the hand every day and in every moment and the more we surrender to this, the more at peace we feel and the more our essence is revealed. It makes the difficult times like power struggles, differences, conflicts and projections, etc. just that much easier to see and resolve. Knowing we are mirrors for each other to use for our wholeness. Our brand together is *Health & Happiness* and we are committed to basing our work and lives on this at the centre point.

What if you are already with your perfect aligned partner but haven't explored this yet?

What if the divine plan wants you to be joined with a partner to support your Calling or even be co-creative in your Calling?

JOURNAL WORK

Are you ready for intimate partnership?

Maybe there's a partner right in front of you who you have not even considered?

What are the qualities you would like to see in this partner?

What do you value the most?

If you are already considering a person, check and see if you shrink or expand in their presence.

# SECTION THREE

## Awareness

*Look at a tree, a flower, a plant. Let your awareness rest upon it. How still they are, how deeply rooted in Being. Allow nature to teach you stillness.* —Eckhart Tolle

The unaware life is a mechanical life, and we only serve our programming and conditioning with very little original thought. The awakened, aware life serves the soul.

Awareness is being alert to the energy field that sits below the content of everyday conversation and living. It is this spaciousness that is our true home. Everything we do is really about coming home to this space inside so we can rest in peace and move outwards from there. In this section we will open pathways of awareness in areas of the soul.

A guest who had been staying with us came into my office and started sharing her story.

Soon she was doubled over in pain and pleading: "I don't want to be hit anymore, don't let them hit me...please don't let them hit me."

I could see she was suddenly a small child who was reliving some terrible encounter. Tears fell down her cheeks and her eyes were stricken with fear.

I gently touched her knee and with a soft voice said, *"Sally, wake up...you're having a nightmare, wake up..."* As soon as she looked up I could see more presence was available and I asked her, *"Is there anyone in the room right now threatening you or hitting you?"*

I looked around the room, motioning her to take a real look. Soon she had to admit, *"No."*

She was a really bright and talented woman and wanted to live her next dream but for some reason during the program she got really triggered and had resorted back to the place where she had been wounded as a child.

Sometimes I wonder how any of us get anything done when we see how intricate a memory and receiving system we have in place. How do we move ahead when constantly we are being triggered and reminded of the past as if it bears any resemblance to our present reality? Yet here it is as bright as day but irrelevant to our path ahead. You can observe people who are honouring their Calling. Watch how much space they have within them. By this I mean, how do you feel in their company? I'm sure you will notice how totally attentive and present they are with you. You will notice a simplicity and peacefulness in their actions. Happiness is something they just are, most of the time.

As you mature, God can use you in new and more significant ways, which is why it is okay to keep letting go and letting God. The tools you use have everything to do with creating awareness because once awareness is aware, you can really see the illusion. You've probably heard the story of a person walking into a room and seeing a snake on the floor. They scream and run back out of the room. Soon they learn it was a rope. They let out a big sigh of relief and chuckle at their delusion. Now they are not going to walk into the same room the next day and have the same experience. They already got that it was not a snake and their perception has changed forever.

By this client bringing her awareness into the pain and the story, she was able to feel it completely while at the same time know it is over. Being abused was no longer true and this was the intelligence she was looking for. By witnessing the arising of this story, it could be fully released. And because she brought her presence into the picture, she was able to meet it with true understanding. Now whenever it arises, there is a knowing of it as something from the past. Something that is not real. Once awareness is aware, you never forget.

When you become aware of 'Yes and Now', you find very few problems and any that may arise in the moment comes with it an intelligence to handle whatever is happening effectively. You are truly never given more than you can handle and this you can trust. Disillusionment of the old patterns you have lived your whole life and grieving and letting go, may be very uncomfortable but with help, you can begin a whole new life.

# CHAPTER TWELVE

# How May I Be of Service?

*"The place God calls you to is the place where your deep gladness and the world's deep hunger meet."*
—*Frederick Buechner*

Your true Calling has to do with some form of service. Whether that is your art, your skill, your talent, your love, or your enthusiasm. Somehow it will bring you into service one way or another.

One day while driving out to the Valley with a friend, we got to talking about being of service. We both felt we knew what that meant, having spent decades bringing forth and working within our Visions. Then, out of my mouth, came these words: *"I'm in service to Angelyn."*

We both looked at each other funnily and paused while we tried to digest what I had just pronounced. Then all the conditioned thoughts came tumbling in like, What? That's selfish. Don't say that too loud, don't even think it, exclaimed the ego.

Next, I said, *"Well, if that is the case and I came to Planet Earth to be in service to this mind/body called Angelyn, then what would I do definitely?"*

Not differently, but definitely.

Again, another pause, while I thought about this statement coming from my core. What would I do definitely?

My first thought was I would write. I would do what I love to do. Ride my horse more and write my books. Then, suddenly and deeply, I felt it. I would love her. I would love this mind/body called Angelyn. I would befriend her.

The awareness of this statement was real, and in that moment, I understood the journey of awakening at a totally different level. I felt the deep and profound love of Self, emanating beyond the body, yet for the body and mind.

This whole lesson reminded me of a little parable.

A traveler wanted to enter a new country and met the King at the gate. He asked permission to enter and visit the King's land. The King said yes, he could, and he would have to honour one task while there. This task, said the King, is: *to love and serve yourself.* The traveler thought it a bit strange but nevertheless agreed, thanked the King, and went on his way. He was a benevolent fellow, and did a lot of altruistic things in the two years he stayed there. He opened orphanages, wrote books, helped people, and kept busy. He figured he was serving himself by serving others.

Soon it came time for him to depart and as he was leaving the country, he saw the King again. The King asked if he'd had a favorable visit, to which the traveler replied, *"Yes, thank you. I opened an orphanage, wrote a book, serviced many people, and kept busy."*
The King did not hear the assignment he had given him from his list and asked if he managed to complete it.
The traveler replied, *"Well, no, I didn't quite have time to get around to that, but I did..."* he started to repeat

his list when the King stopped him and said, *"Well then, it is as if you came and did nothing."*

Wow. Then I got it. I came to love myself first and foremost. And no matter what I do for others, if it doesn't include loving this mind/body, I have missed the point of coming. If I do not do what I came to do, it is as if I came and I did nothing.

I cannot truly love another until I can love myself and if I do not love myself, then I do not know myself. What would I do if I loved myself? Another powerful question to ask.

So, the journey of self-love is the key. From there, the giving is pure. Then the gift offered is imbued with love instead of guilt, martyrdom, or sacrifice. It totally went against my English programming and some of the spiritual beliefs I learned along the way. I had deeply misunderstood the truth.

The suffering in my late twenties with a violent eating disorder helped me learn the body is responsive to the stories the mind tells and the emotions arising through it. Before that experience, I'd never given my poor body this much credit, but since, I have learned the more I treat it with respect and communicate with it as if it were my child, then the less flack I get. I found as I befriended my body, my energy shifted and lightened.

The ego-mind can be the worst enemy of the body and the most violent of tenants. It scolds and criticizes and projects all over the body. When, in fact, the body is benevolent and comes for its own purpose. In a way, the soul is the greatest ally of the body in that it loves and welcomes everything that arises. The ego mind, on the other hand, suppresses, infuriates, judges, and avoids what arises—so much so it barely even has awareness of what arises. It is so fixated on its agenda, which is to keep the sleeping giant sleeping, that it loses all sense of reality.

The mind, the agent of the alleged ego, plays a game of hide-and-seek, which has no relevance to anything evolutionary, only its own survival. The mind wants to keep everything separate and, in so doing, believes it gives itself a task to do. In reality, it wants to rest and the only place it can rest is in the heart. This is when your ego can rest and your soul can illuminate your purpose, your Calling.

So, what would it be like to trust the intelligence of the body? We may as well because it has its journey already appointed. We can struggle with what happens and suffer or surrender and enjoy the ride. The resistance to *what is* causes so much pain and loss of life-force power, whereas falling into life lets it touch us deeply and brings about grace beyond our wildest dreams.

The body loves to be wooed. It responds well to kind words and pampering, not only for the job it has done to carry us forth through this tumultuous journey, but more particularly, because it is the perfect vehicle for this soul's journey. It got selected personally to be the perfect body for the life unfolding through it.

Now, my body is my friend. It is my temple, my vehicle for incredible pleasure and awareness. And ultimately, I am beyond this body. Do I love my body in my more mature years? Yes, definitely. I bow my head to the clarity that flows through difficult life experiences.

When I started living in service to Angelyn, I noticed the focus had shifted. When I Am in service to Angelyn (not the personality but the life force, the creation living as the mind/body known as Angelyn), then this I Am presence serves the world. When this body becomes an empty, abandoned wreckage of programming and conditioning, how can I serve? If I project myself outward to know myself, I blame, judge, and worship, seeking the Self all along but never, ever thinking to look here.

When we wake up and live as the deep well of silence, the ego's job diminishes greatly, and at first, it feels alarming. The ego will work overtime to suggest we are losing our minds and something terrible is going to happen if we break free, but it is the opposite that holds true. We have turned our life around and looked outward for the answers and solutions of living, when all along, they lay within us. As we identify with Self and live from home base, presence arises and touches the heart, and all who come within range get embraced in this grace. So, this body/mind is not who I am but is what I, the soul, lives through.

Like everything, all is a contradiction. It is both and neither at the same time, but don't give up here.

Every explanation I give can only point to the meaning—it is not fully the meaning.

One day, as I saw the illusion, the dream, and I remembered my time with Eckhart when I saw I was not the body or the mind in a meditation we were doing. At one point, Eckhart became a sea of waves and particles and so did the room. I was seeing beyond the physical and it was a shift in perspective. Even though I saw through the illusion, I noticed this body still needed to function fully. It became a moment of seeing this body had its reality, and with or without me, it would do what it needed to do. Cool, so the body has a plan.

**Things to consider:**

- Do you love your body?
- What is your relationship to your body?
- Could you relate to my story of the body? Do you nourish and exercise your body?
- Do you speak kindly to your body?
  Imagine if your body were a child and needed your love and support; your best friend in the world. How would your life be different?

## *How may I be of service?*

So, providing you serve the Mind/Body reality first and foremost, what type of needs in others do you enjoy meeting?

There were two times in particular when I asked the question 'How May I Be of Service?' The first time was sitting on the boardwalk as I shared earlier, and I was told to buy the land behind me and build the retreat centre. The second time was doing a relationship marketing business. In both cases I didn't exactly plan it and certainly didn't have the experience, but the clarity of purpose and timing was unmistakable. Now I can look back in wonder and awe as to the divine plan and how everything relates if we keep moving forward in presence. And as I just wrote that, I laughed, because there is nobody moving forward.

## *How our intuition offers us guidance.*

We may receive intuitive messages, symbols, requests, and ideas that show up in a variety of different forms and through many interesting channels. Understanding these messages and signs may not happen right away. Be with the sign or message until you are drawn into action. In order to be of service, we really do have to get used to being shown what to do and how, sometimes by pretty mysterious forces.

The loudest example of this I ever experienced happened a decade into my relationship marketing business when I was writing a book about the RM industry. I noticed patterns with people's behaviors in my team. Observing people in my business informed my creation of the book From Squeak to Roar—Unleashing the Potential in your Relationship Marketing Tribe. It looks at how people in cooperative teams function and I identified them through sixteen different animals and their characteristics.

As I finished up writing From Squeak to Roar, one thing felt incomplete and was nagging at me. I kept receiving whispers that I had to add the Lynx to the collection of animals, but I kept refusing, not seeing how it related. How do people do RM as the Lynx? This is where it started to get eerie. One day, I received a phone call at my office declaring a huge dead cat lay at OPA, our 1,000-year-old Douglas Fir tree. I ran out to see what nonsense they were talking about and was shocked to find it was true.

Clearly someone must have dropped off this magnificent lynx, as they are not found on this island or within hundreds of miles of here. It lay placed on the knee of the tree with a little smudge pot beside it. I don't think it had been dead too long, and it looked as if it had gotten trapped or injured.

We called the police in to investigate whether it came down to some weird prank or "offering," and both the police who attended, along with myself and two of our community members, felt it harmless and it had simply been placed in our Sanctuary as a place where it would be honored and buried. Perhaps someone found it off-island and thought it should come to Xenia. I guess we'll never know the truth, but one thing for sure, it provided me with full awareness of this message of the lynx.

Regardless, I still refused to add Lynx to the mix, brushing it off as a coincidence. However, I did become a little curious and researched more about lynx.

To my utter amazement, I found I related to its characteristics way more than I ever could have imagined. In fact, it echoed how I did my business so successfully. These resplendent and lucid creatures serve the invisible rules of the game. They understand the act of doing less and achieving more by purposeful actions. Still, no way would I make myself that vulnerable and add it to the book. Even more so, now I had identified myself as the Lynx.

Three nights later, I got woken in the middle of the night with clear instructions: Go to your office and write out your Skype name.

What? No way.

I tried to go back to sleep.

Yes, get up and write out your Skype name, came the instructions.

Dragging myself out of bed and across the hallway to my office, I wrote out my Skype name on a piece of paper. The name I had used for five years— it came from my name Angelyn, and my retreat centre's name Xenia, put together. Promptly, I went back to bed and slept. In the morning, I was curious about it and went back to my office and looked at the piece of paper I had scribbled my Skype name on and there, as plain as day, I saw it: ange**lynx**enia.

Lynx got added to my book immediately.

Life speaks to all of us every day and all day long, sometimes in metaphor, sometimes in messages. We can safely know a higher power guides us if we can simply tune in and act upon the messages. It takes courage to begin, and radical trust to continue.

When I first started living my life with this implicit faith of this inner guidance I must say it took a lot of radical trust because sometimes I was moved in directions I wanted to resist at first. Here is another example of listening and acting upon what I now refer to as instructions:

For the first five years after purchasing my retreat centre I didn't actually live there. I lived on the other side of Bowen Island in a gorgeous three story, 3,000 sq. ft. house with a panoramic ocean view. I didn't really ever expect to live at Xenia, especially since I already had a home.

One day I was working in the Xenia garden doing some weeding when I got this message: You need to be at Xenia. *What do you mean?* I thought, *I am always at Xenia every day.* The message came: You need to be here at night with the owls. I had a sinking feeling in my gut when I considered what this message implied. Where at Xenia would I live with my daughter? There was only the little cabin up on the hill with a small loft bedroom and no power or plumbing. All the other cabins were used for the business.

Feeling resistance swell up in my belly, I tried to bargain with the idea. I could come to work earlier and leave later, I thought. Alas, that didn't cut it and I knew when it came to guidance, it was not up for questioning; it was a direct order.

Funny thing about timing, because just that morning our carpenter Paul was expressing how much he was going to really miss us since he was just finishing up his last job of the dining room expansion at the lodge. He had been working with us for nearly a year and today would be his last day. I went over to him and said he could actually stay and move his tools up to the cabin because it needed to be renovated, so my daughter and I could move to Xenia.

He questioned me: What do you mean? I said I just received a message that I needed to move to Xenia and the cabin was the only place possible for us to move into.

He said, "Well don't you have to think about it first?" He had watched me in the garden weeding and saw I was thinking about something deeply but wasn't sure what.

I said, "No, it wasn't an idea, it was an instruction." I had already been initiated into an inviolable commitment to God's plan.

At first it felt like quite the sacrifice to give up my beautiful big house on the ocean and move into a little cabin in the woods. It would be a major downsize but one we would have to make.

After several months, it was ready for us to move in to. The renovation was beautiful, and we doubled the size of the cabin, giving my daughter her own bedroom and a tree house office for me. It became the happiest place I have ever lived, and still do. It's no longer referred to as the cabin but instead Angelyn's enchanted log home.

If you are new to this idea of listening to a voice in your head you may well want to throw down this book and think I am crazy but before you do that, check in deeply and feel the truth of what I am sharing. It is truth and my commitment is to support as many people as I can to experience radical trust and allow this guidance in. Learning how to trust this guidance is important when you are stepping into unknown territory. And faith and radical trust is not based on a belief you have picked up but from a direct experience you have had. That is where you can really have 100% trust.

**Consider these questions:**

If you were able to hear or sense your guidance, where does it show up in the field of your awareness?

How can you tell the difference between your true guidance voice and the voice of the ego or morphic field?

How do you trust your own knowing? How do you trust your heart?

When you receive a knowing, you know, and it is that simple. This is what you can trust implicitly. But if you have any doubt, learn how to muscle test for truth. I do use pendulums and cards like Collette Baron Reeds[9] cards, which are brilliant.

There is a simple test where you stand up and ask your body if this is the truth. Your body will want to lean forward if the answer is "Yes," or backwards if it is "No." It could also be the other way around, so first establish your body's Yes and No response. Sometimes it is so subtle, but the body knows the truth. It has intelligence and you can trust it.

The voice of guidance is gentle, peaceful, and calm. It is non-judgmental and clear. It whispers and wants to move your body forward. Know the messages from your presence, not your mind. There is a quiet strength and authority to the intuitive voice. It may not be a voice, it could be a symbol, or vision. Sometimes it is a feeling in your gut, or a fleeting thought.

Being held up or back from moving forward. When you are "held-up," pay close attention because it could be for an important reason. I remember one time driving home from Calgary with a friend. We

---

[9] https://www.colettebaronreid.com

were east of Rogers Pass in the town of Golden, having a snack before broaching the difficult stretch of road ahead. The lady in the café just kept talking and talking and literally holding us hostage for "one more story." Listening rather impatiently, everything in me wanted to dart out the door, but I noticed my body wasn't moving. God, why was I even listening to this bullshit story she was telling?

I felt like I was in some slow-motion movie. It was kind of surreal and I couldn't get up off my chair. Finally, it felt okay to leave and off we went onto Rogers Pass and a grueling cold, dark night. At the summit of Rogers Pass, we suddenly came upon an accident that had happened only minutes before we got there. It was a fatal accident and involved five vehicles.

Because we were right behind the accident we got out and spent five hours stopped and connecting with people that needed help. A helicopter landed on the road right in front of us and ambulances made their way through the stopped traffic. It was a very sad night and we will never forget it. When we did the math on the timing, we knew without a shadow of a doubt we would have been smack in the middle of the accident had it not have been for "one more story."

Most things cannot be explained but I do have total faith in the great mystery that guides us. Why did they end up in the accident and we didn't? I have no idea. That is part of the unexplainable great mystery.

As we surrender and trust and almost watch the movie out in front of us occurring in the moment, an awareness starts to arrive, and we find we do not have to be deathly affected by what happens from this place. It's a bit like throwing thick oily paint into the air. Does the air get painted? No. Being the air is the awareness that we are developing. And everything depends on our readiness. The question now is, *Are you ready to take your next step?*

JOURNAL WORK

While routine and structure are good and help us to stay safe, they can blind us to new and important things in our life. Just for fun, what patterns can you interrupt today? Write down some new ways of doing things that have become so unconscious. They can be as simple as sleeping on the other side of the bed or wearing your watch on the other wrist. Having a new point of view changes how you perceive your reality. It opens up new doorways through which you can discover greater authenticity.

# CHAPTER THIRTEEN

# Willingness to Readiness

*"All things are ready, if our mind be so."*
— *William Shakespeare*

In this section we will look at how ready you are in actuality. If you are evaluating the idea of either letting go of your career or moving forward into your Soul Work, it's important to know your level of readiness.

You will recognize yourself in one of these next levels. Willingness and Readiness are two different attitudes – one you can impact, the other seems to be under some cosmic agenda.

Here are the four stages you will encounter along the way:

**Stage 1: Moderately Interested** (toe in):

"A nice idea," or "I think I would like that one day," – (still in the future). To actually branch out and do what you love is in the head as a concept. Maybe it's someone else's idea, not yours. You still like your comfort zone a little too much and are truly nowhere near ready to move forward. You're not in enough discomfort or pain to motivate change but are still kind of interested, though not emotionally connected to it. You may have little or no awareness of the full scope of what you want to create and probably will stop at the first sign of rain because you are not committed - perhaps only with your toe. If you pay really close attention, you will hear the giveaway signs by your inner dialogue as soon as you broach the idea. Tell yourself the truth before you spend more of your life force and years dreaming about something you probably will never do. If you are not leaning forward to the deep end, it probably isn't the right time for this plan.

**Stage 2: Willingness with some effort** (head and toe in):

There is more awareness of your life circumstances needing to change. You may be intellectually aware but still not emotionally aware. Maybe you're feeling a real need to change your situation but still haven't bought into any particular action steps. Your resolve is stronger, and the "willingness" is amped up a little but no decision has been made yet. Some action may begin but it is probably not real unless you get to true readiness.

**Stage 3: Really Willing** (head, heart, soul and most of your body):

You have the attitude of: Tell me, show me what to do and I'll do it. You are persistent and are letting the universe know this is your true intention. You are engaged in the process and taking necessary action no matter how difficult. You show up with commitment. You're clear about why you are doing the work. There is a deepening of your why. You have endurance and you are deliberate in your actions. This is a delicate stage because sometimes you feel you are being tested and you want to quit. You are doing all the right things, but still not fully engaged. You're on the precipice of change though, so don't give up. At this point, taking consistent small steps can yield huge results and more importantly, pop you into Stage 4.

Then seemingly out of nowhere the decision gets made. Some people refer to it as surrender or in a sense, handing their situation over. Then one day, voilà…readiness has arrived.

**Stage 4: Ready** (full body, heart, head, and soul engaged):

Your hand is raised and you are 100% on board. A full-on YES moves through your entire being. Here you experience a complete alignment of the head, heart, and soul. The decision has been made. You may be absolutely sick and tired of the old ways and will do whatever is needed now to change. You know what you want and are emotionally involved. All excuses go out the window. The effort factor is of no consequence because in your mindset, it's a done deal and you will do whatever it takes. You're no longer attached to any old story. It's the end of the old contract. You feel a complete congruency with your thoughts, actions, and results. Where before it seemed so difficult, suddenly grace and ease take over and you are living in the sweet spot. There is still a challenge, but a feeling of excitement comes with it. A quiet knowing that you are on track and all is unfolding perfectly. You are in action.

Readiness (Stage 4) is part of the great mystery and no amount of pushing, praying, or begging can move it or bring it about. I've always said if we could bottle 'readiness' and sell it, we would be billionaires pretty quick. However, we can use it as a gauge to determine where we are at.

Are they ready and willing? Or just willing? It saves us so much time and energy if we tell ourselves the truth. It's not about right or wrong / good or bad, it's the present stage mindset that prepares for what's next.

Surrender is under the jurisdiction of the divine plan. Blind faith or implicit faith – There is a distinction here.

Here is an example to help you understand this:

I met with a member of my team who I didn't know very well, as he had asked me to help him with his new business venture. I sat down and listened to his situation. Even though he had been involved in the business for about a year, he hadn't achieved any success and didn't know if he still wanted to be involved in it. He felt embarrassed talking to people about it and couldn't imagine being successful.

I asked him what he wanted. He didn't know. He said he had made the commitment to do the business twice, but nothing much was happening. He said he was disappointed when the people he thought would love to work with him didn't want to.
I asked him again, "What do you want?"
He said, "To make a lot of money. I thought it would be easy."

I replied, "Yes, you can make a great deal of money but don't mistake this for a get-rich-quick-scheme because it definitely is not that. What else do you want?"

I asked him what he had done before and he said he was a counsellor for many years and he loved it. I asked what he loved about it and he said he loved helping people to make improvements in their lives. Good, I thought, and I pointed out how when he gets a team to work with, he would enjoy supporting his team in a similar way.

I wanted to explore how he could bring who he is and what he's passionate about to his business. We explored other things he wanted but all the while I could feel he had not yet decided to do the business. Eventually I said: "You haven't decided." (Stage Two)

He said he thought he had. After all, he had paid for his initial investment into the business and was using the products himself every month. In other words, because he had made the investment, he thought that meant he had committed.

I said, "No…the reason things are not working out is because you haven't yet decided. And who in their right mind, would follow a person who isn't dyed-in-the-wool to what they're doing? People usually follow someone who is committed and clear about where he is going. Commitment isn't the time you put in but the line you cross. You haven't crossed that line yet."

I shared with him my story of reaching a successful level in my company and I told him how I'd been hovering around the target for five months and presumably I was going to hit it every month.

When asked by my mentors if this was the month – I would always answer "Yes," but something inside was missing and I was not fully engaged. However, on one particular morning, I woke up knowing I was going to do it that month. It arose from within – not from my head as a good idea but from my heart and soul. It had been decided and sure enough it happened.

What was the difference between the earlier months and that month? It wasn't that I was closer to the target from the volume point of view. No, I had been there for five months. It was as if the connection to my heart happened, not just the connection to my head. But how do you access that?, you may ask.

He said, "You mean I haven't decided."

"Yes," I said, "you haven't decided."

"Well then, how do I decide?" he asked.

I said, "You don't…it happens by grace when the time is right. You can prepare for it but you cannot will it."

"What do you mean?" He was puzzled.

"You see it's like my will and Thy will – which one are you working for?"

I wanted to know if it was just about him making a lot of money. What would touch, move, and inspire others to be part of his purpose? Or was it financial freedom for the many? If it was just about him, it was not as motivating but still a worthy plan.

Remember, readiness is not under your jurisdiction; it's part of the great mystery. But willingness is under your control. I can show you how to improve your level of willingness. How to set your intention and the actions you will need to take and things to think about. The more centred in your heart you are, the sweeter it will be. This will prepare you for and hopefully even quicken the decision. It's almost like we think we have made the decision, but we have to know we've made the decision for it to stick. And if you're not sure, look at your results.

You see, I never asked to do relationship marketing. In fact, I was adamantly opposed to it. No, really!! The person who brought me into the business had a very big job on her hands because I told her several times I had no interest whatsoever in doing this business. But through her tenacious commitment and perseverance, she was able to put me in front of her team. She knew my vision and she knew what I needed.

After that, I was on board. And if you were to ask me why I do this business, I would say because I was on the precipice of change and the decision was made before my head got around to it. How do I know that I am supposed to be doing it? Because I am doing it. Apparently my hand was raised. And I finally surrendered to the fact that it was happening regardless of whether I was kicking and screaming and resistant or not. Today this business is not my entire focus but it tucks neatly in to my whole passion and movement of transformation and witnessing people to go for their highest and best.

Think about the times in your life where you didn't want to do something – and you really objected, but somehow it happened anyway. And then a whole new world opened up beyond anything you could have imagined sitting on the outside looking in.

"So, in a way you're off the hook," I said.
He got it right away – he knew it was the truth and in a way it was liberating for him.

He let out a big sigh of relief.

After all what use is beating yourself up or telling yourself there's something wrong going to do? Sure, there are actual practical things you can do to be hugely successful and there are some excellent books that will help. Sure, you can push your way, buy your way, pressure your way, nearly kill your way to success. But your readiness depends on whether it sticks or not. The sweet spot comes with true alignment of purpose and mission that connects with others of shared values. Then you may well experience grace and ease.

So yes, you may be able to make it happen, but usually this approach is not sustainable.

Now once the decision arises – and don't be surprised if it hasn't already happened (even if you don't like the idea), then the job will be how to get over yourself enough to proceed. For this journey will bring up anything in the way of you fulfilling your dreams and offering your gifts and talents to the world

My dream is my retreat centre and working with people to transform their lives and bring their gifts and talents out to the world and get paid for it. I am now living that journey. I am writing books, riding my horse, and because I put the years required to build a great business, I am now reaping the rewards because the business is a vehicle for transformation.

So, how's this sounding so far? What is it you want to do deep in your heart and soul. Now may well be the time.

How do you find out at what stage you are? And if you find yourself at Stage 3, you are on the edge of arriving at your joy and bliss, so keep on going. I want to help you find your readiness.

**Signs of Readiness:**
- You are leaning forward and curious.
- You have a clear vision you are committed to fulfilling.
- You're less caught up in tiny details and fears.
- You have insight.
- You are connected to your essence.
- You are on the precipice of change.
- You are sick and tired of being stuck, bored, unfulfilled, unhealthy, etc.

- You are done with the level you have reached in your career

- You are no longer whining or complaining but are sincerely looking for your next direction.

- You can tell when your heart, head, emotions, and intentions are engaged.

- Objections are minimal. Even if you think you don't have the time or money, you will find ways to overcome any perceived problems.

- You have a strong impulse to act. You do not use excuses or blame anyone or anything for your circumstances.

JOURNAL WORK

Have you ever bought a book and it sits on the shelf at home for years? Then one day, the book falls off the shelf and you read it and suddenly you comprehend the jewels inside? You were ready.

**What stage of readiness do you find yourself?**

# CHAPTER FOURTEEN

# It's One Step Away, Why Won't You Take It?

Failure to thrive is not an option. If you don't go for your dreams and honour your Calling, you may never have to risk failure, but you will have sacrificed your soul. Sure, we can find many ways to numb ourselves and block the gentle inner whisper, but we will never be happy and fulfilled until we step into the unknown and trust we will be taken care of. Trust that what you have to offer and share is significant and necessary for the evolution of mankind. Don't laugh; I'm serious. It is that important.

You may not want to invent something mind blowing or change the entire world on its axis but what is your contribution? It may be a legacy for your family or just for yourself. Ultimately, there is no separation and we are all in this together. But to risk is to live and risk is not knowing how but trusting that you will be shown how. I have learned that the 'how and when' are not under my control but we do need to know 'what.' Your heart knows what your Calling is. We just have to trust and have the courage to begin. One step at a time. We will know when we are at peace with what we are doing.

If you do the exercises and start along this path of discovery, you may stumble and fall and get tested for the strength of your commitment. Don't let yourself be stopped this time. Time is ticking on and if not this time, when will you give yourself permission to come forth and shine brightly as yourself? This is really what your Calling is, to shine brightly as yourself. It is being totally 100% ourselves leaving the rest of what happens through us to the divine plan. It is intelligent and will unfold a path beyond your wildest dreams. Letting go and trusting is all that is required, though I'll admit not easy to attain.

Watch out also for hiding behind your family responsibilities as a way of deferring your Calling into the future. We can often lie to ourselves—or let's say, delude ourselves—into believing our calling is to help them shine brightly in their careers. And this will happen, once you are doing the same.

I know a man who was devoted to helping his wife become the famous singer-songwriter she was abundantly capable of becoming. He worked tirelessly for decades believing he didn't really count because he was living his life as an accountant and figured that was his role. He woke up many years later disappointed that his partner didn't succeed in her career and later realized he was living vicariously through her. Really it was his Calling that was dying on the vine. He could adequately avoid his own path because his programming set him up to think his career was all that mattered, even though it had nothing to do with his Calling.

Sometimes you see parents so fixated on their children and making sure they live their dreams, they sacrifice their own dreams for way too long. Sometimes so long even when their grown kids have flown from the nest they hesitate to even imagine they still have a calling beyond raising great kids. But what if you can have it all?

My daughter and I sometimes reflect how I was able to honour my Calling at the same time as she was able to. Not instead but together, at the same time, and for at least 25 of her 31 years, I have been living mine as well. Did some areas of our life suffer? Yes, absolutely, but I think if you ask her now if it was worth it, she would say we both worked hard and although we had some dark night of the soul years, we have turned out fulfilled and happy we are both living our life's passions now.

We are great cheerleaders for each other and I was never a mother who insisted my daughter did her homework or followed any particular path. I always wanted her to lead the way. I didn't drive her around from one event after school to another the way I saw other parents do. It didn't seem to provide very much down time for kids to relax, explore, or create. I know there are exceptions where kids need to study or do after school events that are aligned to their passion and Calling. In many cases though, it only confuses the child and they become addicted to the pattern of always doing something.

I do not think parents in general give their kids enough free time for creative play and just being in nature. They're overstimulated with programs and homework. I didn't believe in homework and wanted to homeschool my daughter, but she had a clear plan and it would take going to school and university. I was never against education; in fact I love learning. I was just concerned by the way it was dished out and served to kids that needed to learn in alternative ways. And don't get me started on what technology has done to usurp our children's focus and creativity. I'll stop there because that is another book. In fact one I would like to recommend that is right on subject is: Living the Potential[10] – Engaging the Wisdom of Our Youth to Save the World. Renee Beth Poindexter is deeply committed to her Calling in her work with youth and education.

---

[10] Living the Potential – Engaging in Wisdom of Our Youth to Save the World by Renee Beth Poindexter

## Showing up in your Calling.

One day I was driving back home after a weekend away with my partner, who was doing the driving. He announced how much energy he had when usually he was tired after such a long drive. I also noticed how 'up' his energy was. We talked about it and he realized it was because he had spent the weekend aligned with his Calling and he was thoroughly energized by it.

In previous chapters I talked about money and time and here I want to add the energy component. When we are truly aligned with the work of our heart and soul, energy to create is abundant. It feels like time doesn't exist, and we are gobbled up by the experience. All the energy in the world is available to withstand any feat we have set for ourselves. Any energy leakage has to do with our mind and the tales of woe we tell ourselves. Living in resistance takes a huge amount of energy to withstand the walls, bars, and chains created by the mind. In the flow of our Calling we are the energy, we are the movement, we are the space.

You will surprise even yourself when you show up 100%. Make sure you have support around you and particularly with people who will hold your hand and say, Yes and Now. Watch out for people not wanting to affirm you because they are afraid of their own stuckness and don't want to see you break free. You know the story of the crabs trying to climb out of the bucket and just as one of them is about to get free, the others pull them back in? Watch out for those bars you may have put around yourself to limit your boundaries or to keep yourself small. Doing what you are meant to be doing is, in itself, an essential act of healing.

Take time in nature and get used to the silence for it is within the silence you will learn the most.

Do what you do, the way you do it.

Be who you are the way you are.

Find out who you really are now at this juncture of your life.

Watch out for self-sabotage, which is what will happen if you keep hiding. Be audacious and free yourself from the self-created prison. And once you awaken to your Calling, don't go back to sleep.

As Rumi[11] says:

*Don't go back to Sleep.*
*For years, copying other people, I tried to know myself*
*From within, I couldn't decide what to do*
*Unable to see, I heard my name being called.*
*Then I walked outside.*
*The breeze at dawn has secrets to tell you.*
*Don't go back to sleep.*
*You must ask for what you really want.*
*Don't go back to sleep.*
*People are going back and forth across the door sill*
*Where the two worlds touch.*
*The door is round and open.*
*Don't go back to sleep.*

## Be who you are.

*"The privilege of a lifetime is being who you are."*
*—Joseph Campbell*

What if it were as easy as just being who you are? Now you may think that idea is way too simple. How could it be that easy? A privilege indicates it's not for everyone but I beg to differ. It's just that it takes courage to be ourselves, especially when we have

---

[11] Rumi, translated by Coleman Barks, Essential Rumi

lived so far from ourselves in someone else's agenda, we don't even know who we are. Well I'm here to say, it is the right direction.

Two wonderful examples that seared a slot in my consciousness when I heard them were the Larry King and Oprah Winfrey stories.

First, Larry's: When The Larry King Show made its debut, (his dream-come-true career), he was terrified and dry mouthed as he played his theme song, then faded down the music so he could introduce himself. He opened his mouth, and nothing came out, so he brought up his theme song again while he tried to gather himself together. Again, he faded the music and tried to introduce himself but still, not a word came out. His manager stepped into the studio to find out what the heck was going on. Finally, when he did speak, these were his words:

"Good morning. This is my first day ever on the radio. I've always wanted to be on the air. I've been practicing all weekend. A few minutes ago, they gave me my new name. I've had a theme song ready to play but my mouth is dry. I'm nervous. And the general manager just kicked open the door and said: ' This is a communications business!'"

And that's exactly what he did. He communicated his truth and so began his career in 1957. He said he learned a valuable lesson on his first day and that is: there's no trick to being yourself. He was never nervous again after that and went on to great fame and fortune living his Calling.

Oprah Winfrey shares a similar story, thinking she had to emulate Barbara Walters since she was one of her heroes. She learned over time to simply show up as herself and made a fortune and impacted millions and millions of people's lives with her message. Her Calling was literally to be herself in connection and communication with others.

What if that is so for you as well? What if you simply stay in your own lane? If Oprah and Larry can do it, so can you. By doing so, you will attract abundance and live a fulfilled life, having contributed you, your brand, your thing to the world. Imagine if just being yourself was enough?

# CHAPTER FIFTEEN

# It's All Handled

When I say, "It's all handled," it doesn't mean a lack of responsibility or just sitting back on your laurels and being blasé about life. No, it goes much deeper than that.

"It's all handled," means everything unfolds in perfect order, no matter what it looks like on the outside.

Honouring your Calling doesn't mean everything drops in your lap and all of your needs are met. Although usually they are met when you are living your truth this way. But it is in the fear of the unknown that creates the most struggle for people.

In other words, when you have handed it over to a higher power, you must let go and let God, as the saying goes. You may have to sit in the unknown and not know for a while and it's just a matter of getting comfortable with this way of living. And then when you are asked to stand up and take action, you do without resistance or questioning why. Living this surrendered life on purpose may be difficult at times but there is a knowing deep down that you are honouring your Calling. You are on track and on purpose. There is a feeling of alignment no matter what is happening on the outside. Therefore, you don't have to sweat the inevitable. The unfolding divine plan will have its way with you whether you agree with it or not. When you opt in by choice, life unfolds in ways you cannot imagine. Living the surrendered life means witnessing fear and confusion, stress and worry without making it wrong. No need to let it go; just let it be. You will see how it all works out.

Yet at the same time intentionality is very important, giving yourself a "sense" of directorship. I've never been big at goal setting per se, but intention is like a sword or an arrow of truth and all I can say is, if it is aligned with the divine plan, it will happen and if it is not, it will not. No matter how hard you visualize, strategize, and plan. But if you pay very close attention you will feel how life gently moves you. Flowing in that space is profound. Being present as each moment arrives offers a richness beyond any attainment or goal.

To lean in fully to this idea means having implicit faith in a plan that has the road map for your life and a higher viewpoint of the path upon which you travel. This deeper, higher knowing of a plan far greater than you could dream up, unfolds with all its dips and turns and ups and downs, and for whatever reason, a deep knowing it is all handled.

Ultimately, I have implicit faith in a divine plan that I may as well surrender to. If it were supposed to be different, it would have been. No point wondering about what ifs or living with regret. Resisting reality is the biggest way to suffer and I am done with that way of viewing life. I am instead, empowered by leaning into God's plan.

Radical Trust is not about trusting others but trusting yourself, your love, and your connection to God and your inner authority.

You have to trust yourself to stay on your own team and love and protect yourself at all cost, while, at the same time, opening fully to love and the divine plan. It is a dance, for sure, and one worth putting it all on the line for.

When unbidden gratitude starts arising, you know you are on track and on purpose. Sometimes I am simply walking down the pathway to the lodge when this welling up happens from deep within. It didn't happen because I accomplished something, or somebody did something wonderful for me, but just because. Gratitude that arises naturally is a wonderful way to know you are working with the flow of life and the angels.

So, I leave you with the most important directive in this book: Whatever your Calling may be, you have permission to proceed. Listen to what life is showing you and have the courage to say "Yes and Now." Allow yourself to exercise your right and left brain with equal stride. If not now, when?

We need to watch and see and understand the messages surrounding us. If something doesn't flow, perhaps it isn't the right direction or the right time. Check out your readiness levels.

Be the observer, seeing through the eyes of the soul. Forget the noise of the ego and sink deeper into the silence. Embody the silence and you will be home. Listening to all the signs and messages along the way opens up vast realities for you to play within.

Maybe your Calling isn't some new job, business, or legacy but simply being moved by life in total surrender every day.

I feel in my core that I am purely here to be used as an instrument through which the divine plan unfolds, and I know, deep in my soul - *it's all handled.* Could it honestly be this simple? Yes, I would say so. This is how you honour your Calling.

# About the Author

Angelyn Toth is an author/facilitator and founder/owner of Xenia Creative Development Centre on Bowen Island, BC, Canada. Xenia is a beautiful 38-acre retreat centre founded in 1994. It attracts people from all over the world into its spacious and loving natural and delightful Sanctuary.

Angelyn is a Health & Happiness Consultant, established in all of her businesses. She is a top leader in a relationship marketing company since 2005 and values greatly the transformational quality offered in this work.

Angelyn won the Associate of the Year Award for North America for exemplary leadership and was inducted into the Millionaire Club, having personally earned one million dollars in her first few years. She has served on the Field Advisory Board of her company for several years and is the top income earner in Canada. She won the highest award for Leadership, Integrity and Service, the Yun Ho Lee Award.

https://www.youtube.com/watch?v=Rh_LtPBck00

Her own passion for animals and transformation was combined in her book: From Squeak to Roar: Unleashing the Potential in your Relationship Marketing Tribe.

Angelyn has developed a Global 90-Day Program, OPA – Opening Pathways of Awareness, in collaboration with a faculty of conscious entrepreneurs whose passion is to serve people waking up and sharing their greatest gifts in service to humanity.

Her next book: When A Vision Has You, is part of the 25 year celebration of her beautiful Xenia (2019)

Author's photo courtesy of Alexander Brumm

# Thank You

Thank you for reading my book. I hope I opened up some pathways of awareness with you and for you. Subscribe to my mailing list and get posts updates straight to your inbox! angelyntoth.com.

Sign-up now and get FREE access to my recording of The Story of Cabroi, a unique tale of transformation and discovery for children and adults alike. Through the use of metaphor, I will show you exquisite ways to achieve your highest potential.

Check out my web site angelyntoth.com or the retreat xeniacentre.com to find out more about our 90-Day OPA Global Program and other inspiring programs like our silent retreats that will bring you home in ways you may never have experienced before.

## Ways of Contacting Angelyn:

Website: angelyntoth.com

Email: angelyntoth@gmail.com

Facebook: www.facebook.com/angelyn.toth

Xenia Retreat Centre: xeniacentre.com

Published by: xeniacreations.com

Made in the USA
San Bernardino, CA
15 March 2019